In My Father's Words

Sheila Boyd Cook

All scripture verses are from the
King James Version
This book was printed in the United States of America.

To order additional copies of this book contact:

Sheila Boyd Cook
4006 Sweethome Road
Ashland City, TN 37015
615-519-5518

FWB

Cover photo Copyrighted by:
Rick Burgess Photography
Tamarack of West Virginia "Juried Artisan"

Table of Contents

Rev. Terry Lockert Boyd

Acknowledgements

In My Father's Words is just that, the exact words of my father. I felt the title very fitting since the following sermons were transcribed from tapes of my father's sermons. His ministry lasted for over 25 years and this is just a sampling of the great sermons that he preached.

A very special thanks to the Ashland City Free Will Baptist Church for preserving these treasures for me to share and for their love and dedication to our family for those 25 years.

Thank you to my wonderful husband, Joe, who was and is an answer to my prayers. From the moment we met, I knew God had sent him into my life. Thank you for supporting and believing in my desire to share my father's words.

To my mother, thank you for being the role model of a Christian mother, wife, grandmother, great-grandmother and pastor's wife.

Author's Preface

In My Father's Words, is definitely a labor of love. My father spent twenty five years in the ministry and his sermons have help win so many to the cause of Christ. I have spent three years transcribing these sermons from cassette tapes that Dad preached over a span of several years. As a pastor of the Ashland City Free Will Baptist Church for 24 years and pastor of the Horton Heights Free Will Baptist Church for 1 year, his love and concern for people was beyond measure. He shared what the Lord had laid on his heart every Sunday morning, Sunday night and Wednesday night. Dad would spend countless hours in his office preparing for his sermons. As you will discover I have kept the sermons in his own words.

I want to thank the Ashland City Free Will Baptist for keeping the tapes so that I can now share them with you today. Dad's way of illustrating his key points was what set him apart from other preachers. He shared life lessons and life experiences that people could relate to. He often called himself a "country preacher just saved by grace".

1

The Parable of Salvation

Luke 15:3-10

I know we have studied the 15th chapter of Luke in our Sunday school class many times. We have spoken on all the contents of this particular chapter. Everyone talks about the three parables that are found in Luke 15. Let me call your attention to verse 3 and you will find there is not three parables, but only one. Luke 15:3 says "And he spake this parable unto them saying..." and then he gives a list of stories. He changes scenes three times. He tells about the lost sheep, the lost coin and the lost son. It is one parable, on progressive story. It goes from one point and just progresses up the scale. All of it is an illustration of salvation told in simple language.

Luke 15:4-7 tells the story of the lost sheep. Just as an interesting note, when you come to the 15th chapter of Luke underline every word that has to do with joy, rejoicing or making merry. You will find it is continually talking about the sheer love and rejoicing that God has when people come to him. In verse 8-9 he tells the story of the woman who lost the coin. And verse 10 says, "Likewise, I say unto you, there is joy in the presence of the angels of God over one sinner that repenteth.

Love is one of the greatest things in the world. When we talk about love being so supreme, we remember the scripture says God is love. Love is God's greatest gift to the world. Love is the essence of sanity, greatness and happiness. Jesus said, love is the greatest commandment. Thou shalt love thy God. Thou shalt love thy neighbor as thyself. Love is a tremendous thing with God. Wherever the love of God has gone in Christ Jesus lives have been changed and families have been changed. There is a line, that was spoken, I don't remember where, but it says, "When the king stoops to pick up something it must be of some value". When the King of Kings and Lord of Lords stooped from heaven and came to the earth that was cursed, surely he did that for some great purpose. Jesus tells us what that purpose was. For the Son of man is come to seek and to save that which was lost.

There are many kinds of loss. A person may lose his health, his position, a companion or his wealth. There are many things in which a person can lose something. But the greatest loss is the loss of a human soul. For it was that which Christ came to save. Jesus came to seek and to save that soul that was lost. He came to die on the cross to save a soul that was lost. It was his blood that saved souls from sin. So the most horrible use of the word "lost" would be that a soul was lost after all that God has done. Jesus, a few days away from the cross, illustrated the experience of salvation in these stories in Luke 15. The first two verses give us the background for all of this. You see, Jesus, when he was here, loved sinners. He loved them because that was the people he came for. He was kind, patient and had compassion upon the sinner. He even ate with sinners. As Jesus became more and more friendly with sinners the more upset the religious leaders became. They did not want him to have anything to do with those who were lost. To answer the criticism of the religious leaders about his manifested compassion upon the sinners he tells these three stories. They are stories about God's compassion and God's love. Each story leads to a greater one. In the first one there is a lost sheep. The second is the lost money and the third one is a lost boy. A father will sell all of his sheep and all that he's got in order to save his boy. These stories progress and get greater as the time goes on. Let's look briefly at them.

There is the lost sheep. People without God are like lost sheep. This sheep is not worse than the others, he is not a renegade or an outlaw, he is just lost. People get lost the same way as this sheep got lost. I'm sure that sheep get lost through aimlessness and carelessness. I am sure as this sheep began to graze that day he saw the grass getting greener and greener as he looked from one spot to another and he followed that which would satisfy his flesh. He just went where the grass was greener. After he had eaten he became thirsty and stopped and drank from a clear brook and then he laid down to sleep. The next thing you know it was night and he woke up and realized he was alone and lost. People get lost just as that sheep, through aimlessness and carelessness. He did not intend to get lost, but he was simply going after those things that would satisfy him. Finally, he awaken to his situation that he was lost. The scripture says very plainly that it was a sheep that was lost. It is funny how the Holy Spirit dictated and how Jesus used the words that there was no way you could tear down the parable. You notice he didn't say it was a cat, dog or horse that was lost. Any other animal can find its way home, but a sheep can't. Did you ever try to get rid of a dog? You can put a dog in the floor board of your car where he can't see where you are going and drive all over town, drive 10 miles out in the country, and put him out. If you stop by the store to get a coke before you go home, he will be sitting on the front porch watching as you drive up as if to say, where have you been. A cat or a horse can do the same thing, but a sheep has absolutely no sense of direction. The shepherd realizing that sheep was lost would not rest until he did something about it. He left the ninety and nine and went to look for that one sheep. His concern for that sheep is like the concern of God. John 3:16 tells us about the concern God had for us. The scripture says when he found it he came home rejoicing with his friends. Then the scripture tells us, "Likewise joy shall be in heaven over one sinner that repenteth".

The second story talks about a piece of money that was lost. People without God are like the lost money. As long as money is lost it has no value, does it? It is worthless and useless. The only way money can be worth anything is if it is circulated as a means of exchange. That is the only time money is of worth. People who are out of circulation with God and people who are not being used for exchange in the greatest business on the face of the earth are lost. Lives without God are like lost money, they are useless. A person does not have to commit some great sin to be lost. Without God he is already lost. There was rejoicing when the woman found the coin. That coin was worth about a quarter and in that day it would be worth a full day's work. There was great concern on her part. She needed a lamp to find it and when she found it she rejoiced. The Bible says in verse 10 "Likewise, I say unto you, there is joy in the presence of the angels of God over one sinner that repenteth".

The third part of the story is about the lost boy. People without God are like lost sheep, lost money and a lost boy. The word "lost" is a horrible word, isn't it? When I was a boy about 7 years old, I would get up in the morning and just stray like a wild dog. I would hit the road and keep going. Dad was the kind of fellow that didn't worry about you for 2 or 3 days if you didn't show up regardless of how old you were. I got up one morning early and Dad had done something he had never done before. He took out his yellow bone handled knife that he had for many years and laid it on the washstand and went off to work on the farm. The temptation was too much for me, so I picked up that bone handled knife and put it in my overalls and started on my days journey. I caught up with a few boys and we continued walking and ended up a long way from home for a 7 year old. We spent the afternoon playing in a stable on Mr. Turner Walker's farm. I got home a little after dark. Dad came in from the field, washed his hands and said, "Mama, did you see my knife. I lost it or left it here today. I needed it a dozen times today." She said she had seen it on the washstand but that Terry had gotten it earlier that morning. I reached down in my pocket and it was gone. Sheer panic went through me and my heart almost stopped because I knew what I was fixing to get. I had lost Daddy's bone handled knife. Sure enough, he didn't disappoint me, he wore me out. I cried all night and then the next day I got up before he did and slipped out of the house and made my journey all the way back to where I had been the day before. It took me all day. I looked under every rock and behind every tree and bush. When I got to Mr. Walker's wheat field there lay that bone handled knife right where the wheat was nestled down. I was thrilled to have found the knife. I went back home gave it to Dad; he sort of blushed when he realized all that I had gone through to find that lost knife. He didn't apologize; he wasn't that kind of fellow. The next day he traded horses with Mr. Shelton and lost that knife. Riding the wagon that knife slipped out of his pocket. When he got home he told Mama he had lost the knife. I looked him straight in the eye and said, "Yes, and if you were my son I would wear you out". My father didn't think that was the least bit funny. So losing something of value can be terrible.

I have a great deal of sympathy for the lost boy. I know how it is to grow up in a house with an elder brother. Some of you do also. I ran away from home more times than I count. I couldn't stand my elder brother and we fought like cats and dogs. He tried to kill me and I tried to kill him. Daddy always liked him better than he liked me. It was terrible living at home with an elder brother. So I have sympathy for this prodigal son who got to a certain age and said just give me my inheritance. The elder brother received a double inheritance. There was rivalry at home and the fact that the older got twice the inheritance and the younger was ambitious, so he asked for his inheritance and left home. All his ambition turned out to be impractical. He was too much of a dreamer. He was a very restless fellow. Home was too tame for him. He got into situations with a lot of fair weather friends. His judgment was impaired and became lost. He was determined to do as he pleased. He didn't mean to hurt his dad, mom or older brother. He just wanted to go his own way. Didn't Isaiah say that about all of us? Isaiah 53:6 says, "All we like sheep have gone astray; we turned every one to his own way; and the Lord hath laid on him the iniquity of us all". Isn't that the sin of going our own way because we will not have God's way?

There were some signs along the way that ought to have told him he was going to become the prodigal son. First, he was selfish by asking for the inheritance. Secondly, he was lazy by not getting a job. And thirdly, he wasn't very careful with his money. He didn't know the value of money and he wasted his substance. He didn't know it until there was a famine in the land. We see the depths that he went. He was a Jewish boy feeding swine. The scripture says he woke, came to himself and got things straight. He realized he was living in a dream world. He realized he was living in a fool's paradise and it had brought him close to death. He knew the only remedy for him was in the father's house. In Luke 15:18-19 he had planned to say to his father, "...I have sinned against heaven and before thee, and am no more worthy to be called thy son: make me as one of thy hired servants". When he was a far off, his father ran to him, put his arms around him. He brought forth the fatted calf and killed it; brought forth a ring, shoes and robe. There was great rejoicing over the son that was lost but now he was found.

There is a great lesson in these three illustrations of the lost sheep, the lost coin and the lost son. Sinners are close to the heart of God. Sinners are those whom he came and for those he died on Calvary. These illustrations have shown us the concern God has for each of us. Christ came to die on the cross. All that God did and all that Jesus did is to avail until each one of us as individuals come to ourselves as that son did. The father's house was there, the fatted calf was there, the robe, sandals and ring were there. Rejoicing was there. But none of that was his until he came to himself. A good outline for the prodigal son is: he came to grief, he came to himself, and he came to his father's house.

We, like the prodigal, have to come to ourselves and return to God in genuine repentance. Jesus said, "They that be whole need not a physician, but they that are sick", Matthew 9:12. The prodigal son knew he was ill. He knew he was sick unto death. He knew the only remedy for him was to go home. Home was where the need could be supplied.

Prayer: Heavenly Father, we thank you for this privilege of looking again to this passage of scripture. Thank you for the simplicity of the gospel message. We thank you that Jesus made it so plain a child could understand. Just as the coin was lost, the sheep was lost and the boy was lost, they all were found. When they were found there was rejoicing. So it is when one of us who are out of fellowship with you. When we come back there is rejoicing; not only in our hearts, but there is rejoicing in heaven. When one receives Christ as Savior there is rejoicing in the very presence of God. I pray that if there is one here who needs to come to thee in repentance, to receive you as Savior, I pray they will come today. If there is a Christian who needs to move a little closer, make things right and need to come to themselves, I pray they will do that. Have your own way in our hearts and lives and we will thank you for what you do for us, in the name of Jesus. Amen.

2

The Ark of Safety

Genesis 7: 1

"And the Lord said unto Noah, Come thou and all thy house into the ark; for thee have I seen righteous before me in this generation."

The other night at our fellowship supper there came up a shower of rain. It hadn't rained in some time. I guess some folks just enjoy the rain. A number of people were just standing out in the rain. Didn't they have sense to come in out of the rain? I want to talk to you about that. God has always done things in a big way. Everything that God has ever done has been enormous and earth shaking. When God created the heavens and the earth; He made the land, the sea, mountains, and lakes and covered the earth with trees. In the heavens He put the stars, moon and sun. It was all so big and God made it all.

Then when God wanted to save lost man, He did something else big. For God so loved this big beautiful world that He had created it to live together in harmony and peace. But that world had become fallen and polluted. God so loved that big world that He gave his only begotten Son that whosoever believeth in Him shall not perish but have everlasting life. His Son came and died for redemption and opened the doors of heaven and said whosoever will let Him come.

The gospel is big. Heaven is big. The invitation includes all who will let him come. With that we are prone to forget God in any other aspect of his being. He was big in creation and big in his invitation for men to come into his wonderful heaven. In the matter of judgment, God also did big things. God had to deal with an enormous situation and the judgment that God brought upon the earth was a big all inclusive judgment. In Noah's time, the scripture tells us that sin was filling up this big world that God had created. People were wallowing in their sin and every one of them, with the exception of one family that God found righteous, had turned their backs on God. Wallowing in sin, turning away from God, who had created the whole thing, and God's patience became so exhausted with man that He said, I will destroy the earth. It repented God that he ever made man. He said, I'll destroy the whole thing. I will wipe it from the face of the earth. Big in judgment included the whole world. Every living being with the exception of eight perished. God opened the fountains of the deep and the windows of heaven and the floodwaters began to rise until the whole world was covered and all perished with the exception of eight.

Let's step back just a little bit. In the midst of all that sin God found one righteous man; one godly man by the name of Noah. He gave the invitation to Noah because Noah was that type of man who could teach his family the ways of God. That is why he was chosen, because he could take the commandments, statutes and ordinances of God and command them to his children. God selected him. God told Noah to prepare to build an ark for the salvation of the species of animals. When God brought all the animals into the ark, God said to Noah now you and your family come in for thee I have seen righteous before me in this generation. Noah did as God commanded and all those who were on the outside of that ark of safety perished from off the face of the earth.

This world in which you and I are living is fast filling up with sin. This world has been exhausting the love and patience of God since the days of Noah. God's wrath is filling up. The world is filling up with sin and God again has prepared an ark of safety. God has given his Son for our redemption. He says to all who would repent of their sin and come to Jesus Christ, there is an ark of safety. The flood of judgment is soon to break upon the face of this earth. Judgment is coming as sure as there is a God in heaven; as surely as the Bible is the word of God and surely as Jesus is the Son of God. All of those outside of Jesus Christ will perish. Judgment is coming. As it was in the day of Noah, so shall it be in the days of the coming of the Son of man. God's cup of wrath is full and about to tip over. The world is filling up with sin. God has prepared an ark as in the days of Noah. The ark of safety is God's Son.

Paul tells us in Romans 8:1, "There is therefore no condemnation to them which are in Christ Jesus, who walk not after the flesh, but after the Spirit". I want us to see three things from this passage of scripture. First, man is lost. Second, men have every opportunity to be saved. And thirdly, there is only one way to be saved. One of the reasons missionary enterprises are lagging and church membership is status quo and one of reasons there is no more separated Godly living among the saints of God is the fact that men have lost the ability to believe that men are lost. They have lost the belief that God can send a man to hell and condemn a soul to burn forever. Men are lost outside of God. In the days of Noah, the scripture says, speaking of God, the end of all flesh is come up before me says God. Because of what He saw, He passed the sentence of death on the world and its inhabitants. Do you know we are living in a condemned world, today? Do you know the world in which we are living is under the condemnation of God? We are condemned because of sin and condemned because of the rejection of Jesus Christ. I know that is contrary to modernistic preaching. Other people would tell you that all is peace. I believe it was Jeremiah who said that the men cry peace, peace and then sudden destruction came upon them. There is no peace. Conditions are worsening. The world is not getting better.

People are not getting better. We are not growing up. We are not shedding our growing pains. Satan is still the prince and ruler of the air. He stills rules and reigns in the heart of man. This age, as in the age of Noah, shall come before God in judgment.

Do you believe that? Do you believe we are living in a condemned world? Do you believe what God said about the world in which we are living that it is hastening to judgment? That is what he told Noah and the world in Noah's day. They laughed at Noah. That is what God is telling us in our day. Do we laugh at God today? II Thessalonians 1: 7-8 says, "And to you who are troubled rest with us, when the Lord Jesus shall be revealed from with his mighty angels, in flaming fire taking vengeance on them that know not God, and that obey not the gospel of our Lord Jesus Christ". Do you believe that? Do you believe there is coming a day that the Son of God shall be revealed from heaven? He will come to this earth with vengeance and help from his mighty angels and shall pour forth the wrath of God to those who do not know him and obey not the gospel of Jesus Christ, do you believe it? I believe it because God said it. It is hard to get people to believe that they are lost. Folks say they are just not that bad. They are lost, not because they are good or bad, but because they have rejected the only Savior which is the Lord Jesus Christ. You can give your body to be burned. Paul said, if you reject Christ as Savior it avails you nothing and you are lost outside of God. All of those outside of the Lord Jesus Christ are on their way to judgment and on their way to an eternity in hell. If people could believe they are lost, they would cry out, "What must I do to be saved." Men are lost. The Bible says the wages of sin is death. The soul that sinneth it shall die. There is none righteous no not one. There is none that seeketh after God. He that believeth on the Son shall not be condemned, but he that believeth not is condemned already because he hath believed not. Lost because he believes not; not because he has committed murder or did some terrible act. He is lost because he believes not and rejected the Lord Jesus as his personal Savior. In the days of Noah there must have been a lot of good people lost. There were some good mothers and fathers in the crowd who perished. There were good neighbors in that crowd who perished. Men who lived good moral lives, who paid their bills, but they were lost just as men are lost today.

Secondly, they had every opportunity to be saved. Noah preached for 120 years. His theme was judgment is coming, prepare to meet thy God. It was the same message Amos preached. It was the same message that all of the Old Testament prophets proclaimed and the New Testament disciples, apostles and preachers proclaimed. Judgment is coming, prepare to meet thy God. The people laughed at him. Surely, he must have looked like a crazy man out in the wilderness building a ship because it had never rained. God gave them 43,800 days to repent. Folks say today, when a young person dies, that God was unfair. Their reasoning for that is he didn't live long enough to live his life for God. Whether you live to be 20 or whether you live to be 100, God has given you an entire lifetime to prepare. He gave them 120 years, but they turned down every opportunity. Many today are doing the same thing. They have had opportunities by the thousands to identify themselves with God and God's people by believing on his Son, by repenting and confessing their sin and accepting Christ as Savior. They turn down every opportunity. God has given you another opportunity today. What will you do with it? God said my spirit will not always strive with man. Those people, in Noah's day, had folks who prayed for them. Noah was a righteous man and prayed for those who were lost. There are folks today that have had people pray for them. Prayers have been lifted up on your behalf. They have been lighted to the very throne of God that your salvation would become a reality. If you continue in sin and reject the Lord Jesus Christ, those prayers which have been prayed on your behalf will serve only to press you deeper into hell.

What kept them away? I would imagine the delight they had in worldly pleasures. The pleasures of life were so thrilling to them that they drowned out the voice of God. I believe that others meant to be saved tomorrow. Yes sir, first thing in the morning, I'm going to Noah and say Noah put me down, I want to come on board the ark. The first thing next week or as soon as my children get through college, as soon as I get the house paid for, as soon as I get a little older, I am going to identify myself with God. Most people that plan to get saved at 12 o'clock die at 11:30. They intended to. Is that your trouble? Are the things of life so thrilling to you that you have drowned out the voice of God? Do you intend someday to receive Christ as your personal Savior? Let me tell you, you may think we are all a bunch of sticks in the mud. You may think those things give you pleasure and they do for a while, but honestly if you will turn your back on those things that give you pleasure and dedicate and commit your life to the Lord Jesus Christ, he will give you a joy that will last for eternity. It will start today and you will know what real joy feels like. They had every opportunity, but they waited too long until God himself shut the door of that ark. They came and plead for mercy and Noah said, God had shut the door. Jesus said that when God shuts the door, no man can open. So they perished. Today, men have everything imaginable to draw them to Jesus Christ. If I were going to go to hell, I'd want to go to hell from the darkest point of Africa. I wouldn't want to go to hell living in the United States of America. I wouldn't want to go to hell living in a city with a church on every corner proclaiming the gospel of the Lord Jesus Christ. We have church with open doors on every corner inviting people. All of us have folks who have prayed for us from our earliest life and are continuing to pray for us. We have had folks to weep for us to God. We have all had the Holy Spirit to teach and nudge us and tell us we are not living right and to teach us to respond to God's invitation to receive Christ as our personal Savior. All of us have had times of sorrow we had to endure that made us look up and contemplate God for a moment. We've had sermons, songs, everything imaginable to draw us to Jesus Christ. A man has to climb over all of that to go to hell.

Then finally, men are saved in just one way. I think all of us are prone to get a little liberal in our theology. Some of you have been prone to say, well after all we are all serving the same God. After all we are all going to the same place, our ways are just a little different. I want to tell you something, I came out of a church that believed they were the only ones going to heaven. I've gotten more narrow minded than that and believe some of them aren't going to make it. Did you know that Free Will Baptist have the only way? We have the only way to heaven. We are not the only ones that have it, but we've got it. There is only one way to heaven and that's through the Lord Jesus Christ and that is what we preach; that is what the Assembly of God preach, and the First Baptist, and Nazarene preach. There is only one way and we've got and a lot of other folks have it too. There is just one way. Folks have been saying heaven is like a big city. There are all kinds of roads that lead to the city, but after all, we all get to the city. Some go the interstate, some go the state highway, some go the county road, some go up the river, some go up the creek, and some fly in. Eventually, we all get there. Heaven is not like that. There is one city that is not like other cities and that's the holy city of Jerusalem. It's just got one road to get there and we all walk that same road through the precious blood of the Lord Jesus Christ. Jesus said, I am the way, the truth and the life, no man cometh unto the father except he come by me. They either go their way and go to hell or go God's way and go to heaven. Many good people perish because they were outside the ark. All of those outside of Jesus Christ are lost. When Adam and Eve sinned, God did not come down into the garden and say to them, I want you to be good from now on. I want you to do the right thing and be sincere about what you do. That is not what God said. He said there is only one hope for you and all of lost humanity and that is the seed of women. What a picture of salvation we find in Adam and Eve. When they sinned they knew that they were uncovered and they went out and made garments to fit themselves and were alright with that. Men have always been proud of their robe of righteousness, of goodness and morality. But God said it is as filthy rags. God came to that garden himself, slew an animal, shed his blood, and took the skin and covered Adam and Eve teaching our first parents that there is no atonement for sin, no covering of sin, without a substitute giving his life for that sin. Without the shedding of blood there is no remission of sin.

What a plan. That is the gospel in a nutshell. We have sinned. We are all guilty before God. There is absolutely nothing we have to cover our sins before God. God must do it all. God has done it all. He does it all with Jesus Christ. He is our only hope and ark of safety. I'll say to you today, knowing that I will be laughed at just as Noah said, judgment is coming. You have heard that over and over again. I say it to you again, judgment is coming. God will pour out his wrath upon this world in which you are living. It is a condemned world and you're not safe to walk on it. And you laugh and turn away from that alright, I have done all I can do but I intend to do, what Noah did, I intend to bring my wife and my children on board with me. That is all Noah accomplished in his whole life preaching. No one got saved except his daughters, their husbands and his wife. Let me tell you, he was a success. When a man can come on board the ark of salvation and bring his family with him, he is a success in God's sight. I intend to go on board and I intend for my wife and two girls to come with me. The invitation to you is the same as Noah gave to those people, will you join us on board the ark?

Prayer: Our heavenly Father, we thank you again for the privilege of having the Holy Spirit tug at our hearts. Father, we praise you this morning for the ark of safety which thou has prepared for all who would believe. We thank you it is a place of safety, security and a place where no man can turn us away. It is a place we can be safe when you shut the door. Help us Father to know we are on board. Help us to know we are in your keeping. Father, I pray today if there is anyone who has turned away every opportunity to come on board that they would shun it all today and risk being laughed at, being called a fanatic, risk whatever man might throw at them to be in the place of safety. Father, teach us there is one place safe for our souls and that is resting beneath the shed blood of the Lord Jesus Christ. Father judgment is coming, thy word has proclaimed it for all to believe. Help us to apply our hearts unto wisdom that we might not be lost. Father, speak to hearts today and if there is a need for salvation, I pray that they might come. If there is a need for rededication, I pray they would come. Whatever the need Father, we leave it in your hands and commit it to thee, believing in the name of Jesus. Amen.

3

The Invitation

Isaiah 55:1-9

"Ho, everyone that thirsteth, come ye to the waters, and he that hath no money; come ye, buy, and eat; yea, come, buy wine and milk without money and without price. Wherefore do ye spend money for that which is not bread? And your labour for that which satisfieth not? Hearken diligently unto me, and eat ye that which is good, and let your soul delight itself in fatness. Incline your ear, and come unto me: hear, and your soul shall; and I will make an everlasting covenant with you, even the sure mercies of David. Behold, I have given him for a witness to the people, a leader and commander to the people. Behold, thou shalt call a nation that thou knowest not, and nations they knew not thee shall run unto thee because of the Lord thy God, and for the Holy One of Israel; for he hath glorified thee. See ye the Lord while he may be found, call ye upon him while he is near: Let the wicked forsake his way, and the unrighteous man his thoughts: and let him return unto the Lord, and he will have mercy upon him; and to our God, for he will abundantly pardon. For my thoughts are not your thoughts, neither are your ways my ways, saith the Lord. For as the heavens are higher than the earth, so are my ways higher than your ways, and my thoughts than your thoughts."

In this particular passage of scripture God is issuing an invitation. An invitation that is as good as God is powerful and extended to whosoever will. An invitation to all men everywhere to come and partake of salvation or happiness and everlasting life. He goes on to talk about the fact that he urges all men everywhere in the light of this glorious invitation he has given, to forsake their wicked ways and return from their backsliding and come through this invitation to God and God will abundantly pardon and bless those who will come. He closes the passage by saying my ways are so much above your ways and my way of thinking is so far above your way of thinking. As far is heaven is from the earth so is God's thoughts from the thoughts of man. Therefore, God is issuing the invitation to come and accept that which God has given and to accept the promise and provision of God and enter into an everlasting covenant with God; which ensures salvation. If you would ask the question today to the average man about God; what is God, who is God, and what is his relationship with men today. Ask them what is salvation and how it works. You would hear man's thoughts about God and his thoughts about salvation. Man's thoughts are so much less than God's and usually the answer you would hear would be in opposition to what the word of God has said. When you say to people today, God is still the narrow God; he is still the God of one way, people refuse to accept the God of one way. They say it is too narrow and that man must have the freedom to move within God's guidelines and hence make his own decisions. Yet God is very strict. God has provided one way. He has provided one standard. God has given one answer to man's problem. Men prefer to have another way. Men prefer to interpret the scripture that they can decide for themselves and not what God has said. Man has set up certain standards. For example, we have a standard of time. When you say to a man it's 12 o'clock, they don't say I want it to be 11:45 or 12:30. It is too narrow to say it's 12:00 and I'd have no choice. Let me have it my own way and I'll make up my own time. Men don't do that. Men have standards of sports. When you are playing baseball you get three strikes, that's a standard. When I go to bat and say I don't want it that way, I want four strikes or don't count any strikes at all on me. No, you live by man's standards and you don't argue with those standards. We believe that a pound is 16 ounces. You may say don't hold me to 16 ounces, I may want 18 ounces. Man lives by the standard man has set.

When it comes to God's standard, men say I don't want it that way. Let me have another way. In God's love and wisdom he designed that standard for our benefit and for our blessing. God did not design standards that we might be brought under subjection or that he might show his power, but he did all of that for our good. In the book of Deuteronomy chapter 6 verse 24, I underlined one verse of scripture and refer to it often. When he gave the ordinances to the children of Israel Joshua spoke and said, it is for our good always. Let's think about the fact that God is a God of just one. God is God and beside God there is none else. Isaiah 45: 5-6 reads, "I am the Lord, and there is none else, there is no God beside me: I girded thee, though thou hast not known me: That they may now from the rising of the sun, and from the west, that there is none beside me. I am the Lord, and there is none else". That is God Jehovah, the God of the word and yet men will not have that standard of one God.

Men have many gods. For example, there is the god of the evolutionists who believe that God was the first cause of everything here and let everything here evolve. They believe in evolution to show their intelligence and they add enough of God to it so they won't be called atheist and end up with nothing. They know God is some kind of first case. They do not know God as the loving, heavenly father, the creator of all things as we know him. There is the God of the modernist who says I believe parts of the Bible. I believe that the Bible contains the word of God. That is, there is some in there that is not the word of God, but his word is contained in there. They say, I'll choose which to believe and which not to believe. There is the god of the legalist who believes they will be saved by keeping certain rules, rituals and ceremonies. But the Bible says there is one God. He is the God who created us all. He is the God who is the father of the

Lord Jesus Christ and the God that so loved the world that he gave his only begotten Son. He is the God that loves all of us, saves us and keeps us. He is the God all of us must, someday, face.

Then there is one Savior. There is a kind of philosophy that is gaining strength that believe all men everywhere are the children of God. The responsibility of Christians is to simply notify them that they are children of God. That God died on the cross to save all men from sin and our responsibility is not to bring men to salvation but to notify them of that great act in God that they are now saved and are now children of God. Yet the Bible makes it very clear that is not true. In Act 4:12 the Bible says, "Neither is there salvation in any other: for there is none other name under heaven given among men, whereby we must be saved" John 1:12 explains how to be members of the family of God. "But as many as received him, to them gave he the power to become the Sons of God, even to them that believe on his name:". All men are not children of God. There are men who are children of the devil. The only way we can become members of the family of God is to be born into the family of God through faith in the Lord Jesus Christ. Men in their natural state are lost. All men are lost outside of Jesus Christ. If all men were saved and children of God, and if God had so designed that all men would go to heaven there would have been no reason for Jesus to have come in the first place. There would be no reason for him to suffer and die. The angel said to Joseph, and she shall bring forth a son and thy shall call his name Jesus for he shall save his people from their sin. The angels said to the shepherds, for unto you is born this day in the city of David, a Savior which is Christ the Lord. ... The first message from heaven was there is a Savior. This is the one Savior and the reason he has come because all men are lost. God so loved us that he gave that son to die for us on Calvary that we might be saved. Jesus said of himself, I have come to seek and to save that which was lost. There is one God, one Savior and one way of Salvation. Jesus said, I am the way, the truth, and the light. He did not say I am a way, a truth and a light. He made it very plain that no man could come to the father except by him. Only Christ can bridge the gap between God and man. The Universalists says today that God is a divine God, but that God is a loving God and a good God. Because God is good and loving, all men are saved. The Bible says that is a false premise. When the Bible says the wicked shall be turned in to hell with all the nations that forget God; they say God is too good to send a man to hell. God in his love could not possibly condemn a man to eternal suffering. Yet, God, in reality, does not send men to hell. Hell was prepared for the devil and his angels. Men are determined to go and God said the wicked shall be turned into hell with all the nations that forget God. The Bible continues to say whosoever was not found written in the Book of Life was cast into the lake of fire. Did God mean that? Was God trying to scare somebody when he talked about hell? God was not trying to scare anybody. God meant what he said. There is a place prepared for the devil and his angels and the wicked shall be turned into that place.

There are two destinies that face every man at the end of his life. One is to live for the Lord Jesus Christ and enter into everlasting life with him in heaven. The other is to enter into everlasting life with Satan and his angels. Some would say that salvation is a mixture. It is a mixture between what man can do and God's grace. That if man is good enough and does enough good works, God will bless his efforts with mixing enough grace with that until all men because of their goodness and the grace of God will be saved. There is only one work that is necessary. The scripture says this is the work of God that ye believe in him whom he hath sent. That is our work.

There is one God, one Savior, and one way of salvation and there is one mediator. Some people believe that God is so far off and so high above us that we have to have someone to go for us to the presence of God and that is true. We do have to have someone mediate between us and God. Man cannot mediate for us before God, the priest cannot mediate for us before God and

Mary cannot mediate for us before God. What does the Bible say? I Timothy 2:5 reads, "For there is one God, and one mediator between God and men, the man Christ Jesus;" That mediator is Jesus Christ our Lord. Man said we don't want that narrow way, we want to have a multitude of mediators. God is far off and I do have to have a mediator to go with me and present my partitions to God. That mediator is Christ. When I was a little boy my father was rather quick tempered sometimes. I never was smart enough, like my children were, to figure out when to go to him. My father could be laughing and hit you all the same time and never change expressions. I never figured out if it was a good time or not, so I had to go through my mother, and then she went to Dad. By the way, that is the way my father ruled the house. Everything was condensed and it all went through mother back to us. If Daddy said, Terry needs a whipping, mama had to do it. He would tell her to tell us something. Mother was a condenser. She sifted it through her condensing feelings and then it got to us. I had to have a mediator to go to my Dad. The same is true about my heavenly Father. I need someone to go before me to God. Jesus Christ is that one. There is only one alternative. If you don't come to the Lord Jesus Christ, there is one alternative for you in this life and in the life to come. The Bible says there is only one thing left for you and that is to spend eternity in hell without hope. There is only alternative in this life. Men are searching for what the word of God gives. They don't know what they are searching for, but they are searching for happiness, contentment and fulfillment. That is exactly what the word of God gives.

We can either follow the Lord Jesus Christ in our earthly life and a full blessed life or we can live our lives always searching for happiness. The one alternative in life is to bow to God and what he has said about us and find that life that's lived in fullness or to be miserable all our lives. I have preached for a long time and I never did like to try and persuade and try to linger in the invitation. I never liked to convince someone beyond their will to accept Christ. I believe, at least my personality allows me to preach the word of God, issue the invitation and leave it to God without twisting arms or forcing. But for the last year there have been those individuals that I have had the privilege to minister and witness to and those individuals have slipped out into eternity and more and more I'm finding myself saying, I wish I had tried a little harder; I wish I had urged that individual a little more. Maybe I should have prolonged the invitation and maybe that person would have been saved before their lives were taken.

There is one God, one Savior, one plan of salvation and one alternative. I present that God to you. I present to you the God who has made the standard, not that he might crush you but that he might bless you. If you have never accepted this one God through the one Son, the Lord Jesus Christ, I urge you to do it today. I plead with you to accept Jesus Christ as your personal Savior. I plead with you to come by the one door, the one way and the one son and have him bring you to the one God. If you have accepted Christ, but through the years, the philosophy of the world has sort of distorted the picture of God and his Son, I urge you to come back to that one Savior and one God.

Prayer: Heavenly Father, we thank you today for the privilege to study another portion of thy word. We thank you that the word is plain. Father we thank you that we believe in the literal interpretation of the word of God. That we believe there is one God and beside thee there is none else. We believe that you so loved us that you gave your only Son. I pray that if there is someone who needs to accept Jesus Christ as their personal Savior that they will receive him. If there is a Christian that needs to rededicate their life to the Lord, I pray you speak to that heart. Accomplish your will and we will thank you for it in the name of Jesus. Amen.

4

Five Tragedies of the Church

Acts 20:28-32

I suppose that nothing exists today that is not under attack. Someone is attacking everything. Someone is always out to stop progress. Someone is always out to defame people of good reputation. Someone is always out to get even. Someone is always out do something harmful. One of the greatest attacks is against the church of the Lord Jesus Christ. I tell you the church is not exempt from criticism. The church needs to be criticized. The church needs to have some people stand up and say this is what we believe the church ought to stand for. The church, church nationwide, is becoming polluted. It is, in fact, losing its message to the world. The reason it's losing its message is because many of the bigger churches that have the most money, people and resources at their command, have long since lost the message of salvation and no longer make any impact upon the world. Others have simply become polluted. I know is must grieve the hearts of a lot of good Methodist people to know that some of the great Methodist Universities have used publically avowed homosexuals to teach in their seminaries and their Bible Colleges. It must grieve the united brethren's heart to know that they were the first to ordain homosexuals to preach. It must grieve a lot of good Baptist to know there are a great number of their people working in the gay task force. So the church needs to be criticized. The church needs more people like Anita Bryant.

The church needs men with guts to stand like she did, and make a stand.

The church of the Lord Jesus Christ was one institution that was so dear to the apostle Paul. It was the one institution that Paul gave his life for. That was one of the reasons Paul endured so much persecution for the sake of the church of Jesus Christ. God had revealed to Paul the mystery of the church. Because Paul understands God's working in relationship through the church and to his people, Paul was willing to undergo all that prosecution. He believed in the church of the Lord Jesus Christ.

Acts 20: 28-32 says, "Take heed therefore unto yourselves, and to all the flock, over which the Holy Ghost hath made you overseers, to feed the church of God, which he hath purchased with his own blood. For I know this, that after my departing shall grievous wolves enter in among you, not sparing the flock. Also of your own selves shall men arise, speaking perverse things, to draw away disciples after them. Therefore watch, and remember, that by the space of three years I ceased not to warn every one night and day with tears. And now, brethren, I commend you to God, and to the word of his grace, which is able to build you up, and to give you an inheritance among all them which are sanctified." The apostle Paul loved the church. It was the dearest thing to Paul's heart. He compared the church of the Lord Jesus Christ to three things. First, he called the church of God a building. This reminds us of Jesus Christ as the foundation of his church. Then he referred to it as a human body with arms, legs, eyes and ears, remind us of the function of the church. What the church is to do and how it is to function. Then in Ephesians, Paul wrote that beautiful letter comparing the relationship between a husband and wife to the fidelity and love of the church of Jesus Christ which is his bride. The mystery of the church had been revealed to Paul by the Holy Spirit. God had shown to Paul that it was through the church that God intended to work for the individual redemption of men and women. So Paul loved the church.

Paul began to make some predictions about the church. He said there would come times of great tragedy in the church of the Lord Jesus Christ. He said there would come times of great difficulty in the church of our Lord. He said the time is coming when men who call themselves members of the church shall rise and begin to speak perverse things and get disciples for themselves. We have seen that come to pass. Paul said the time will come when men from the outside, the unbeliever, shall come into the church as roaring lions and grievous wolves, trying to destroy the church. A lot of people today say the church has out lived its effectiveness; that the church is on its way out. But it through the church of the Lord Jesus Christ that so many people have come to know the Lord. It is worship services where so many have had the Holy Spirit speak to their hearts and they have turned away from sin to receive Christ as their Savior. The church is the place that God intended to use to mature and develop his own people.

The sweetest place on earth to me is the church where the gospel of Christ is preached; and where people who believe the Bible gather together; and where the power of God blesses that relationship. Paul said some tragedy would come to the church; difficult times would come to the church. I would like to share with you some of the tragedies that have come to the church.

The first tragedy is the unattended church. The majority of people in this world belong to somebody's church, synagogue, cathedral or group. Yet there are precious few who attend the church with any kind of regularity even though most of the people are members. As you drive through our state you notice that people are building bigger and bigger more beautiful church buildings. Everyone has a building program it seems. Bigger, more beautiful convenient churches yet fewer and fewer people are attending regularly. I believe that Sunday morning the church service is a big blow out, Sunday night is a little turn out and Wednesday night is practically a fall out. Do you know what would happen if all the churches in the world would build their churches to accommodate the Wednesday night prayer meeting crowd? We could set up a pup tent and we wouldn't need a church building. When the First Baptist Church in our community got a new pastor a few years ago, he was a dear friend of mine. Bro. Hester was one of the finest pastors that had ever pastored in our city. He went on visitation and knocked on a door not too from this church. He introduced himself and perhaps they didn't listen closely to what he said and where he was from. The person told Bro. Hester he went to church. Bro. Hester asked the man where he attended church. The man told him he attended the First Baptist Church. "Really", Bro. Hester said, "you go to the First Baptist Church". Bro. Hester continued to talk to the man and told him he heard the church was a good church and the pastor was wonderful. The man replied, "He is a wonderful man, definitely a man of God and I love to hear him preach". Bro. Hester asked the man to give him the name of the pastor and the man gave the name of a preacher who was at the First Baptist Church 20 years ago. All this time, the man was talking to the pastor of the church he said he attended.

The Bible tells me that I am to support the church of the Lord Jesus Christ. I am to support it with my financial giving and to pray for the church. But the main thing is to be faithful in attendance to the church. "Not forsaking the assembling of yourselves together after the manner of some is; but exhorting one another: and so much more as you see the day approaching" Hebrews 10:25. What does the Bible mean by those words? In the last day there will be a tendency to become a member of some church in name only. Forsaking the assembling of ourselves together as the day of great tribulation approaches more and more of God's people need to be coming together. In these last days, church attendance ought to increase rather than decrease because we are going to need the strength we get from one another and from the word of God. I believe a fellow ought to go to church twice on Sunday. I believe he ought to go to Sunday school and church. I believe he ought to go once on Sunday night and Wednesday night. If he is in the choir he ought to be there to rehearse with the choir. God calls his people to be faithful. Revelations 2:10 says, "...be thou faithful unto death, and I will give thee a crown of life." Paul says as the day approaches, increase your church attendance. A revival, if it is to come to the church, will be characterized by an increase in attendance in the church.

The second tragedy of the church is the unbended knee. E.M. Bounds was one of the greatest Methodist evangelists that ever lived,was a man saturated by the power of God. He said the only thing he had ever received that had any good to it was the result of prayer. Everything that had ever happened to him in his ministry, in his church, in his relationship with his family that was good, was a result, direct or indirect, of his prayer life. When you do what people tell us today, increase our learning, we get what learning can do. When we increase our education, we get what education can do. But when we pray we get what God can do. Failing to pray is a tragedy. That great day in the church, the Day of Pentecost, was a result of prayer. That day when God's people were quickened by the giving of the Holy Spirit was a result of prayer. God's people came together, 120 of them, and they prayed for 10 days and Peter preached for 10 minutes and 3,000 souls were saved. Today we meet together 10 days, pray 10 minutes and wonder why folks don't get saved. Jacob never amounted to a hill of beans until he learned to wrestle with God in prayer and he became the prince of Israel. Prince with God: he became Israel, as a result of prayer.

The third tragedy of the modern day church is the unread book. I am talking about the Bible. There is no question that you believe the Bible. You can ask a Free Will Baptist if he believes the Bible to be the inspired word of God and he'll hit you over the head with it, brother. He believes that the Bible is the inspired word of

God. We believe in the book. WE are Bible believing people. Our tragedy is not liberalism. It is not the fact that there is some professor in some college out there who is living in sin and trying to drag other people down with him. The tragedy is we believe in the book and don't read it. We do not saturate our hearts and our lives with the precious word of God which we believe so strongly. If the preacher doesn't read the word of God daily he is a backslider. If the minister of music doesn't stay in the word of God, he is a backslider. If a Sunday school teacher doesn't stay in the word of God, he or she is a backslider. If the church members don't saturate themselves with the word of God and stay in it they are backsliders. The tragedy is not reading what God has to say.

A mother watched her little girl as she was stricken with an incurable disease. She watched as her daughter died within a matter of days. A few days later, the pastor went to that home and asked for the Bible that he might read to them some comforting scriptures and they looked and looked and finally found the word of God. When the pastor opened it a wasp nest fell out. As he began to read the scripture, the mother began to weep and said "my daughter never heard what God had to say. She never heard me or her father read what God has to say to her in his word; she never heard us pray".

We send our children out into an antagonist; unbelieving, godless, atheistic world never having heard what God had to say. They never hear mom or dad pray or read the Bible. We wonder why they are not stronger than they are and fall before temptation. The Bible is a love letter. Did you ever see a teen-age girl get a love letter? The mailman comes and the girl goes running to the mailbox and she finds that little love letter with SWAK written on the back. I used to write a few. In fact, I wrote a lot of them. In fact, I wrote love letters for other boys to send to their girlfriends because I was good at it. I could say some of the sweetest things. The girl gets the letter runs into the house.

She tells her mom she got a love letter today. But she goes to the living room, puts it in a magazine and decides to wait till next year to read what he had to say. Is that what she does? No, she goes to her room, slams the door hops on the bed tears it open and reads it, and reads it over and over again because it is a love letter. That is what God's word is to us – a love letter.

The fourth tragedy of the modern day church is the unconfessed sin. When I was growing up, I was taught that you had to sin and I did. I was taught that it was normal and that you sinned every day. I quit preaching a sinning religion a long time ago. I don't believe in a sinning religion. I don't believe in sinless perfection nor do I believe in the fact that Christians have to sin. I believe we have the perfect atonement for sin. I believe we have the perfect sacrifice to cleanse us from the power of sin not only the penalty of it. I believe that if we do sin that we have an advocate with the Father. I believe that the blood of the Lord Jesus Christ cleanses us from all sin. And I don't believe we can live a life where we never sin. Can any of you say that from the time you were saved to this day, you never committed a sin? If you can I'd like to have your name and enroll you in the local liars club. John said if we say we have no sin we are a liar and do not the truth. So we all do sin. The tragedy of that there is unconfessed sin in so many of our lives. We have an advocate with the Father. The blood of his Son cleanses us from all sin and unrighteousness if we only be faithful to confess that sin he is faithful to forgive. We block the channels of God's power because we will not confess the sin in our own lives.

The Nazarene people believe in sinless perfection. They believe in sanctification. Some of my best friends in the world are in the Nazarene church and I kid them a lot of times about sinless perfection. They believe they don't sin anymore that they have been sanctified. That's alright if they want to believe that. I said to one of them, "you are a sinner". He replied, "No, I'm not." "Yes you are, the Bible says everybody is a sinner". They said, "No I have been sanctified so therefore I don't sin". I told them I could prove they were a sinner. "How?" they said. "You just got mad as the dickens with me didn't you?" Yes, I did was their answer. "The Bible says to get mad is sin so you are a sinner just like the rest of us", I stated. How many of us have unconfessed sin in our lives; sin of the flesh, sin of disposition, sin that we have not confessed to God.

Finally, the fifth tragedy of the church today is unexpressed love. I think this is probably the greatest tragedy of the church. We don't show our love as we ought. I think it is good for people to show their love. I think it is good in a family for mom and dad to show that they love one another. I think it is good for the children to show that they love one another. For some silly reason we have got to the point where we believe that if we show any kind of emotion or love that we are called emotional or weak.

We are so afraid of getting out on a limb that we don't even bother to climb the tree. We don't want people to label us over emotional especially in our churches. We dare not become emotional in our relationship with Jesus Christ. I have never preached when people shouted and jumped over pews and all that stuff. In fact, it would probably scare me to death if they did. How many times have you been in a church service when it was so dry and the Spirit of God was so far away from that place and the preacher was preaching on the danger of emotionalism? It would have been dangerous to strike a match. Don't beat on the pulpit; watch that emotionalism it will get you in trouble. It will lead you into all kinds of doctrinal imbalance. Brother, I believe it is good for a child of God to put his arm around somebody's neck and say brother, I love and appreciate you and what you do. I love you in the Lord. It is good for us but we don't express our love to one another. Because of that people can sit in a church today dried eyed when they are hearing from the word of God that which ought to make the saint of God shout and rejoice. We don't weep anymore. The reason we don't weep is because we don't want to disturb anyone. We don't want to be broken hearted and express our love.

When was the last time you expressed your love to God? When was the last time you simply got alone somewhere and you just told the Lord you love him. Lord, I love you. I am glad the Lord is strong because if some of us did that it might shake the Lord up. To express our love to the Lord would do you good.

Have you told anyone in the church lately that you love them? Did you know that pastors like to be told that you love them? Isn't that funny? Isn't it strange that a pastor would like that? Silly, I guess but they do. They love to hear folks say, I love you. Sunday school teachers enjoy being told they are appreciated for the fact that they spend hours studying to teach you on Sunday. When was the last time you told your Sunday school teacher you loved and appreciated them? Many a pastor has resigned from his church and moved because he never heard anybody say, brother, I love you and I appreciate you. He thought he was failing because no one ever expressed any love or appreciation. Many a Sunday school teacher has quit teaching because they never heard one word of appreciation and love by their students. They thought they failed and felt they were not affecting anyone's life so they quit. It doesn't hurt anything to tell people you love them.

I believe that revival can come to our church when we fall in love with each other. I think there ought to be some loving going on when the saints of God get together. I think there ought to be some forgiving when the saints of God get together. But I think there ought to be a lot of spiritual foot washing going on when the saints of God get together.

The tragedy, Paul said, is coming. People will drop out of church; they will quit praying and reading the Bible. They will quit confessing their sin and they will quit expressing their love one for another. If you want revival in your soul and in your church increase your church attendance, confess your sin, increase your Bible reading and prayer life, increase your appreciation for other people and your expression of that to other people and you will see revival.

Prayer: Heavenly Father, we love you because you first loved us. When we were astray seeking to do our way and our own thing you came to seek and to save us. It was not that we sought after thee, but you sought after us. With your love you captured us. Father, we love you because you were willing to die for us. You were willing to stoop down from glory and pick us up. Father, we thank you for what it cost to redeem us. We pray that you will help us, as your children, to see and know and understand the mystery of the church. Help us father to realize it was purchased with the blood of thy son. Help us to realize it is that institution dearest to the heart of our Lord and Savior. I pray that we will cooperate with you and your church for the redemption of men. Father, help us as children of thine to be able to simply love one another, for God is love. Help us to show the community God through our love for one another. May we be like the disciples and the people said see how they love one another. Help us to return to the book. Helps us to return to our knees and send revival in our hearts, our lives, and in our church. If there is one here who does not know you as their personal Savior, I pray that today would be the time they receive Christ into their heart. If there is a Christian who needs to move closer to the Lord, I pray that they come in repentance and rededication in their lives. Bless us and we will thank you for what you do for us, in the precious name of Jesus. Amen.

5

Being Reconciled to God

I John 1:3 Leviticus 17:11

I John 1:3 reads: "That which we have seen and heard declare we unto you that ye also may have fellowship with us; and truly our fellowship is with the Father, and with his Son Jesus Christ."

Leviticus 17:11 reads: "For the life of the flesh is in the blood: and I have given it to you upon the altar to make an atonement for your souls: for it is the blood that maketh an atonement for the soul."

The Old Testament, as you know, is divided into three sections: the Law, the Prophets and the Writings. The section entitled the Law is the very heart of the law found in the book of Leviticus and the very heart of Leviticus is chapters 16 and 17. The heart of chapters 16 and 17 is verse 11. The heart of the book of The Prophets is Isaiah, the heart of Isaiah is chapter 53 and the heart of chapter 53 is verse 6. "All we like sheep have gone astray, each one to his own way and the Lord hath laid upon him the iniquity of us all." The New Testament is divided into the Gospels, the Epistles and the Book of Revelation. The heart of the Gospels is the book of John and the heart of John is chapter 3 verses 14 – 16. "And as Moses lifted up the serpent in the wilderness, even so must the Son of Man be lifted up. But whosoever believeth in Him shall not perish but have everlasting life. For God so loved the world that he gave his only begotten Son that whosoever believeth in him shall not perish but have everlasting life." The heart of the Epistles is the book of Romans, the heart of Romans is chapter 5 and the heart of chapter 5 is verses 6-11. "For when we were yet without strength, in due time Christ died for the ungodly. For scarcely for a righteous man will one die yet peradventure for a good some will even dare to die, but God commended his love to us in that while we were yet sinners, Christ died for us. Much more, then, being justified by his blood, we shall be saved from wrath through him. For if when we were enemies, we were reconciled to God by the death of his Son much more being reconciled to God, we shall be saved by his life. And not only so, but also joy in God through our Lord Jesus Christ by whom we have now received the atonement."

In all of these verses, the shed blood of the Lord Jesus Christ prevails. It is the heart of the Law, the Prophets, the Gospels, the Epistles and it is even the heart of the Book of Revelation. The shed blood of the Lord Jesus Christ, someone has said, is the pearls of God's revelation that was put together on the thread of Calvary. All the way through scripture the very heart is the saving and shed blood of the Lord Jesus Christ. In fact, if these declarations are not the very heart of God's revelation and God's reaching out for the souls of man, then the Bible is just another book and Christianity is just another religion. But the heart of the book is God reaching out after the soul and proclaiming the gospel that saves the soul from sin. In every instance, in the proclaiming of the coming Messiah and the looking back to the coming of the Messiah, looking forward to the cross and looking back to the cross, the very heart of all of that was without the shredding of blood there is no remission. The very heart of God's revelation to man is the shed blood. The blood doctrine is the basis, not only of Christianity, but it is strangely enough the very basis of the Jewish religion. At the very heart of what the Jews believed and practiced as their religion there was the blood. The blood was the only way to God. In the Old Testament, no man could come to God empty handed. He had to come by way of sacrifice. He had to come to God by way of some innocent victim suffering, dying and shedding his blood for him in his place. In the Old Testament, the Jews had to have a sacrifice, not only a sacrifice, but a blood sacrifice. These victims offered up for sin had to be offered up on a certain altar, a certain way, and on a certain day. There was no other way the sacrifice was pleasing to God. In the New Testament, the regulations are stated in a more definite way. No one can come except by the blood. Not only does it have to be a certain kind or a certain time, but it has to be a certain kind of blood and it was the blood of the Lord Jesus Christ. Despite the teachings of modernism on this particular point, we stand or fall as Christians by the saving power of the shed blood of the Lord Jesus Christ. If John was right when he said that the blood of his Son cleanses us from all sins, then Christianity is right. If John was right when he said if we confess then God is just to forgive them, there is salvation. If John was wrong then the whole Bible is wrong. Christianity rests upon the fact that God so loved the world that he gave his only begotten Son, a sacrifice, the shedding of the blood of his Son – that is the basis of Christianity. We do not base our faith on the goodness of man, we do not base our faith upon the goodness of God, but rather we base our faith upon the shed blood of the Son of God who gave himself for us that we might live a life pleasing to God. Then if that is true, if the shed blood is essential, everything else that man can do is of no avail. All things, as far as salvation is concerned, amount to nothing in God's sight, if in fact, what John stated is correct. If blood is required, then baptism is not enough. If blood is required then right living is not enough. How many times have you heard people say I am alright the way I am? I go to church and was baptized. But if the blood is essential and John's statement is correct and if the word is correct when it says that without the shedding of blood there is no remission of sin, then church membership is not enough. If the Bible is true then baptism is not enough, right living is not enough, human rights is not enough, compliance with some kind of human creed is not enough. Only the flowing cleansing blood of Jesus Christ will avail.

It is necessary that all of us apply our hearts unto wisdom to see whether or not we have been to the cross of Jesus Christ and there appropriated the grace of God to our very souls. If nothing else is enough, if not being guilty of grievous sins is not enough, if it is not enough to be baptized or sprinkled or immersed or living right then it must behoove us to know whether we have been washed in the blood of the Lamb. Have we been to Calvary, as the song says, and have we found ourselves in the redeeming grace of God?

Do you know beyond any shadow of doubt that the blood has been applied to your soul? If there is any doubt or if there is any fear or uncertainty then the Bible warns us and invites us to flee from the wrath to come. By accepting God's offer of salvation, we must confess our sins and place our faith and accept him as our personal Savior. The promises in the Bible of the blood run throughout the whole Old Testament. In the book of Genesis, just when God is beginning to open his revelation to us he says, "And I will put enmity between your seed and the seed of the woman. This signified all the way back to the third chapter of Genesis that he would send the Messiah. When he is come, he will bruise the serpents head and he also signified in that verse of scripture that the Messiah would be born of a woman and would not have an earthly father. He also says that he would be that sacrifice for the sin of mankind. Isaiah said, "We did esteem him stricken smitten of God and acquainted with grief. Who bore our sin, who bore our grief and our sorrow on the cross? In every detail, beginning in the book of Genesis until the ending of the revelation of God in the Old Testament, every ritual which brought man into God's presence in a redeeming sense, the blood was applied. God was the initiator of it. He told them what kind of animal, what day and what alter. He was the one who looked over it and gave every detail of it. Remember when God said to Moses that he wanted him to sacrifice and told him exactly what kind of sacrifice to be made. He told Abraham the same thing. God even ordained the priests and God even said to the Jews in the Old Testament,

"When I see the blood, I will pass over you". God was giver of the sacrifice. In the New Testament, it is even clearer that Jesus Christ was the Lamb of God. God provided him. God provided the lamb. God provided the very altar of which the Lamb of God was sacrificed. God initiated it all and all of it was a promise that God had given to us in the Old Testament.

Today, we wonder, after realizing that the days of the Old Testament are closed, about the power of the blood. Does the power of the blood still have the same kind of power? Does the blood have the same kind of cleansing power that it had in those days? We ask ourselves the question, "what does the death of Christ have to do with me today? What does the shedding of the blood of Jesus Christ over 2000 years ago have to do with me? The Bible makes it clear to us in the new covenant that it was that blood of Jesus that reconciled us to God. The scripture, speaking of Jesus Christ when he was on Calvary's cross said, "God was in Christ, reconciling the world unto him and hath given unto us the message of reconciliation." That means that God and man were enemies with one another. They were estranged from one another. That enmity prophesied existed in seed of man and the seed of God. God came down and in the person of his Son, the Lord Jesus Christ, on Calvary's cross made it possible for sinning man and a holy God to be reconciled together and then he said I have given unto you the ministry of reconciliation. It means you and I have the responsibility of pointing to the lost and dying world the dying Savior; and say to the whole world this is your sacrifice, this is God's Son dying for you. Therefore be ye reconciled to God. Come and bring your sin. The scripture says God was in Christ reconciling the world unto himself, not imputing their trespasses unto them.

Paul said, "For it made him sin who knew no sin that we might become the righteousness of God in him". Unless we are righteous, we cannot go to heaven. Unless we are as righteous as the Lord Jesus Christ, we cannot go to heaven. How many of us could say if the Lord Jesus Christ were standing beside us, I am as righteous as the Son of God? Yet, the Bible makes it clear that unless we are as righteous as Jesus, we cannot go to heaven. Isn't it wonderful that the scripture says God was in Christ reconciling the world unto himself, not imputing their trespasses unto them." And then it makes that wonderful statement that we become the righteousness of God in him. It is not our righteousness that gets us to heaven, but his righteousness is imputing unto us. We stand in the righteousness of Jesus Christ. For it pleased the Father that in him should all the fullness of the godhead dwell and having made peace through himself and by him I say, whether things in earth or things in heaven and you that were sometimes alienating him in your mind by your wicked works, yet he hath now redeemed in the body of his flesh through death to present you holy and unblameable and unreprovable in his sight.

Isn't it wonderful to know that not because of our righteousness, but because of our faith Jesus Christ can present us to God unblameable? How many of us can stand in God's presence by ourselves and not be blamed. But Christ presents us before the Father unblameable, as we accept him as our own personal Savior. There is one message that I would like to get across to everyone in this community, if I could live long enough to do it. So many times when I talk to people, they talk about their goodness. I remember one time a fellow saying to me, "I don't go to church because that is the day that all my children visit and I am sure God understands." I am sure God did understand. I assured him that God did understand. I said, "I am not saying God approves, but I can certainly tell you for a fact that God understands why you don't go to church." If I could get one message across to every sinner, it would be this: "If you are not reconciled to God, then you are an enemy of God. You do not straddle the fence. You are not in come kind of limbo state where God has not yet made up his mind. Christ said, "Who is not with me is against me and scattered before me". If we are not reconciled to God, the scripture makes it plain that we are enemies of God with no hope and no promise.

Jesus on the cross provided a way and if we have not come by that way, if we have not come by Christ, to walk freely into the presence of God, then we are yet alienated from God and are enemies with God. How many times have you heard someone say and you understand perfectly what they meant but they say, "I have made peace with God". I have talked to people just before they died and I have had them say to me, I have made my peace with God and I know what they mean. But brethren, you cannot make peace with God. Jesus Christ makes peace with God for you. God was in Christ reconciling the world unto himself. It is Christ who makes peace for us. We dare not stand in our own presence but ask Jesus Christ to be our perpetuation for sin. His blood reconciles and redeems us. The scripture says you are not redeemed with corrupted things such as silver and gold, but by the precious blood of the Lord Jesus Christ.

One day, the Bible says to us, that it will be that blood of Christ that will welcome us into heaven. In Revelation 7 John saw that multitude before the throne, many people of many tongues, of many nations, of every tribe under heaven and John said who are they? The Lord said they are they that have washed their robes in the blood. They are those who have come to the great tribulation having washed their robes in the blood of the Lamb. Have you been reconciled to God? Is God satisfied with your life? Are you an enemy with God or have you been reconciled through the Lord Jesus Christ? Do you know the Redeemer? Do you know him as the Savior of your soul? If you do, the Bible makes it clear that there is no penalty hanging over our heads; "for there is now therefore, no condemnation to them that are in Christ Jesus that walk after the Spirit and not after the flesh". The promise of the blood, the provision of the blood and the power of the blood is available. Be washed in the blood.

6

Two Relationships with God

I John 1:6 – 2:2

One of the greatest blessings that can come to mankind is to become part of the family of God. One of the greatest curses is the fact that we aren't acting like young'uns. If we are a child of the king and if God is our Father, it is time we started acting like God's kids. I am glad to be a part of the family of God and I am glad that I have brothers and sisters like you to share in a most wonderful and beautiful relationship in this family of God.

There are some things that have bothered me a great deal. I suppose that it is one thing that every pastor has to learn and that is to avoid heartache and heartbreak. We have to realize that everyone who says Lord, Lord is not a Christian. You have to come to a place where everyone who makes a profession of faith are not members of the family of God. There are many who have made a profession of faith, who started out in service to God and have long since fell by the wayside. They think that the pastor does not care. They think that the church does not care. They think no one is concerned. I am convinced that you cannot convince a person to do what he already knows he ought to be doing. I think those who are members of the family of God ought to be in God's house. They ought to be fellowshipping with other brothers and sisters in the same family. It bothers me when I see that they do not. One of the things that sort of upsets me a little bit is the fact that there are those who claim to be children of

God; who claim to be in the family of God but who show in their lives no evidence whatsoever of the new birth.

The story of Lot bothers me when I read the wickedness Lot did and the Bible calls him a righteous man. I have never been able to adjust that in my thinking. We have people in our own church and in our own community that say they are a Christian, but who are living in open and fragrant sin. They show no evidence, whatsoever, of being saved. Are they saved? If they were to die after making that profession of faith sometime back, would they go to heaven? Are they in the family of God?

There are two relationships that I want us to understand. I want you to turn with me in your Bible to 1 John 1:6 – 2:22. I want us to try to picture, if we can, and get a clear understanding of two relationships that every Christian has with God. It is very vital and critical that we understand these two relationships that every Christian has with God.

The first relationship we have with God is the matter of being in the family of God. Becoming children in the family of God is relationship one. But there is another relationship that is the matter of having fellowship with God. How many of you are in a family here on earth do not have the best of fellowship with your brothers and sisters, mom, dad, etc.? You see there is a possibility of being in a family but not have fellowship with that family. If we can see these two relationships, it will go a long way in helping us understand some things about God and his relationship to us.

Let's talk about the family of God for a moment. As I said, one of the greatest privileges we have is to escape from the corruption of the world; to escape from being orphans to becoming into a family – one that has the same interest, share together their blessings, defeats and everything else -to be a part of something. I talked to a man not long ago and he said, "I am a Christian. I am saved and have been baptized. I have never been to church but once in my life." He was an older man. He continued to say, "I don't believe in going to church". I said, "You are not a part of the family of God, brother". "Oh yes I am", he said, and there is a place reserved for me in heaven. I just don't believe in church." I then asked him what he was saved from. You are saved from sin, but what are you saved to? You were saved to a fellowship with God and God's people. I went on to say to this elderly man, when you were born to your mom and dad some 60 years ago, did they leave you out in the yard? Did they ever say don't come in his house? When you were born into your earthly family, you came into the house. When a person is born into the family of God, they will find their way to the house of God. They don't stand out in the yard; they come into the house.

When we talk today about people being saved, we use particular terms to identify a child of God. We say that individual has been 'born again'. That term is being used like the word 'Christian' until it no longer means anything. We know what the words 'born again' mean. We use the term 'a child of God' or the term 'being saved'. Why do we use those particular terms? Because we have learned that mere profession does not mean possession. We have come to know that because a person says he or she is a Christian, doesn't mean they are. Even if a person comes to an altar and prays, doesn't mean he is a Christian. The fact that someone has their name on a church roll does not mean they are a part of the family of God. So we use terms like 'born again' and 'saved'.

There are a multitude of people in this town Methodist, Baptist, Pentecostal, etc. who have their names on the church roll who are not a part of the family of God. You may say, preacher, that's pretty harsh preaching. Are you saying that within our church there exists that condition? Yes, that exists in our church and we ought to face it. We ought to expose it; not for the purpose of hurting someone; but for the purpose of healing. Exposure should be for the purpose of allowing the Holy Spirit to come and deal with that particular situation. Most people think when they are exposed or when God exposes some sin in their life it is for chastisement sake. God does not expose sin that he might hurt us, but that he might heal us. I am glad that God exposed some things in my life now rather than wait until I get before him and then expose sin. I can deal with it now. We need to deal with the fact that all those who say they are a Christian are not necessarily a part of the family of God.

In Matthew 7:21-23, Jesus said, "Not everyone that saith unto me. Lord, Lord, shall enter into the kingdom of heaven; but he that doeth the will of my Father which is in heaven. Many will say to me in that day, Lord, Lord, have we not prophesied in thy name? And in thy name have cast out devils; and in thy name done many wonderful works? And then will I profess unto them, I never knew you; depart from me, ye that work iniquity." It is interesting how from time to time we have evangelistic campaigns. We go out into the community and take a census to find out how many people are Christians and how many are not. How many attend church and how many do not? I'll tell you the truth, why we do a census? It is not to get together a lot of religious information, it is to find out who you can go visit and hope you can win to the Lord. That's why you do it. We try to find out who is and who isn't. The greatest prospect roll, I think Billy Graham said this, is its own members' roll. The greatest mission field for any church is among its own members. Do you realize what would happen if every member of the Ashland City Free Will Baptist Church or any other church, would show up for Sunday morning worship; after the preacher had a heart attack and after the ushers went crazy trying to find seats for everyone? Do you realize what would happen if everyone who is a member of a church in this community were to show up for church? There wouldn't be enough folks to run the Dairy Dip. I'll tell you why folks stay open for business on Sunday because we Christians patronize them on Sunday and keep them busy and make them money.

Gipsy Smith, who was a great evangelist, was in fact, a gypsy. He knew gypsies. He lived with them and he was one. He knew a gypsy by just looking at them. He went to a gypsy camp one time and saw this beautiful woman. She was dressed like a gypsy and acted like a gypsy, but there was something peculiar about her. He began to question her and she finally said she couldn't fool him. She was not a gypsy, but had just joined. If a lot of church people were honest they would have to say, I am not a Christian, I just joined. They had the yearly round up and I came in, I joined and that is their relationship to the church. There is only one way to be a child of God. There is only one way to become a member of the family of God. You can't become a member of the family of God because your mothers or fathers were Christians, or because you're the preacher's daughter or because you are the deacon's son. There is one way to become a member of the family of God.

Nicodemus in John 3:1-21 came to Jesus and ask the question, if we could paraphrase, how can I become a member of the family of God? Jesus said Nicodemus you were born one time to your mom and dad on earth and that is how you became a member of your earthly family. To become a member of the family of God you have to be born into the family of God. You have to be born again. Nicodemus was confused and said how can I be born again? Jesus began to explain to him the new birth. How many of you know you can't explain the new birth? You have to give the Holy Spirit freedom to let us experience it. It is something you cannot explain; you have to experience it. Nicodemus, I believe, had that experience. He did it like all of us have to do. The first thing you have to do in order to become a member of the family of God is to be convicted of sin. John tells us that the Holy Spirit is come to convict the world of unrighteousness, of sin and of judgment to come. Jesus came to die on the cross that we might have salvation and the Holy Spirit came to quicken that to our understanding. You have to be convicted of sin. You have to say I am a sinner. Folks don't like to say they are a sinner. Did you know they are the only people that qualify for heaven? Sinners are the only ones who qualify for heaven. Jesus said to the Pharisee, who said they were perfect, you don't need me. Those who are well don't need a doctor. I am come to seek and to save that which are lost. If you are lost, you are a candidate for heaven, if you will let Jesus save you.

The second step is to repent. Luke 13:3 says, "I tell you, Nay: but, except ye repent, ye shall all likewise perish". There can be no salvation outside of conviction and repentance of sin. I want some of you to notice something for me. Some of you are followers of particular television evangelists. I want you to listen to them preach. I want you to list the times when they mention a salvation without repentance and without conviction of sin. People are preaching a salvation without repentance and there is no such thing. It doesn't exist. Except ye repent ye shall all likewise perish. So we come into the family of God first by being convicted of sin, repenting of that sin and then to go to him for forgiveness.

A little boy made him a flipper. Some of you are old enough to remember the flippers. Where you cut up the inner tube of a tire and put it onto a crooked sassafras fork. The little boy went to his grandma's house with his flipper and the old goose was standing out on the edge of the pond. The boy took a bead on that goose and let the rock go from that flipper hitting the goose right between the eyes. What was he going to do? Grandma would kill him for killing her goose. So he took that goose and went out behind the stable dug a hole and buried it and turned around and his sister was standing there looking at him, she said, "I have got you where I want you". The next time it was her time to carry in the water, he carried it in. The next time she was to bring in the stove wood, he brought it in because he was being blackmailed. One day he had enough and went to his grandma. He threw his arms around grandma and began to cry like little boys will try to get sympathy. He looked up and said, "Grandma I killed your goose. I have lived miserable ever since I killed your goose". Grandma replied, "Son, I knew you killed the goose. I was looking out the window and saw you kill it. I have just been waiting for you to come to confess". That is the way we are with God.

Isn't it a wonderful thing to know that you have been forgiven? We have to have the burden lightened. WE have to know we are free from sin and the sheer joy of forgiveness. As many as receive him, to them gave he the power to become the sons of God. And the moment that happens, a miracle takes place in your heart and you are born again into the family of God. Something about being in the family of God you bear certain characteristics. I see some people and look at their nose and can tell what family they belong to. We do bear certain characteristics of the family. If you are a member of the family of God you bear certain birthmarks. The first one is you enjoy family cooking. We have some of the best cooks in this church and I thoroughly enjoy our fellowship suppers. Some of you have traveled around the world and tasted delicacies, but you say to yourself, "If I could just get back home and get my feet under my table and enjoy my family's cooking". The food in the family of God is the word of God. A lot of folks don't like to hear you talk about repentance, conviction, sin or hell. If you are a member of the family of God you hunger and thirst after the word of God.

Liberalism has failed. It took over by leaps and bounds contaminating a lot of our churches. It is on its way out, brother, because there is no message of salvation in it. People who know God hunger and thirst after the word of God. Secondly, to be in the family of God you love the furtherance of the family. It just thrills your soul when you see somebody get saved and see the family enlarging. I remember when my little sister was born. I didn't even know I was expecting. Daddy took me to the creek one day and I knew something was up when he went swimming with us. We were supposed to be in the tobacco patch pulling suckers, but dad said we could go swimming. I came home from swimming, jumped up on the bed; mom caught me and pushed me back into the floor. She pulled the covers back and there was that little girl. "Where did she come from", I said. I was so thrilled that our family, as big as it was already, had another member. That is how I am when folks get saved here in our church. I love to see the family enlarge and members added. Folks who are in the family of God love to see it also.

Thirdly, to be in the family of God, you love fellowship. I John 1:3 says "That which we have seen and heard declare we unto you, that ye also may have fellowship with us: and truly our fellowship is with the father, and with his son Jesus Christ". Fellowship is a particular Christian word. It means to have things in common, to share. Did you ever notice how some of the civic organizations use the word fellowship? It doesn't belong to them. It is a Christian word. You see some club advertising a get-together for a time of fellowship. What they mean is you are going to have embalmed chicken and green peas like bullets and a bunch of old stale jokes. That's what they mean. Fellowship is a Christian word which means share together a common interest.

Giving is a part of fellowship. You ever notice these minister's of music just before the offering, how they try to get the congregation in the mood for the offering. I've been to some churches where the minister of music just goes crazy just before the offering asking everybody to stand and shake hands with your neighbors. You don't have to do all of that to the children of God. People who are a part of the family of God get a blessing out of giving. I was in a situation one time when I just know that the church treasurer was going to get a dead buffalo out of the offering plate. Folks squeeze a nickel so hard before they turn it loose. People of God enjoy giving because it is a part of fellowshipping with God.

Finally, there is a thing about fellowship. You can say I'm a member of your family but you have to have a birth certificate to prove it. There is a thing about being in the family of God and having fellowship with God. People sin. Christians sin and we have the atoning blood. The scripture says we have an advocate with the father which gives us the victor. There are a lot of Christians who die saved, who are in the family of God, but are out of fellowship with God. I am convinced there are a multitude of Christians who are out of fellowship with God. They are out of fellowship with God because of sin. Sin has separated them from their fellowship with God. David prayed and said, "If I regard iniquity in my heart, God will not hear me." An example of that is Lot. II Peter says Lot was a righteous man. If I were the judge Lot would have gone to hell. I'm glad I'm not the judge. The Bible says he was a righteous man. I suppose that means he was a saved man. He was out of fellowship with God. He pitched his tent toward Sodom. He put his eyes on the world instead of heaven. He put his time and his talents into materialism of making a living instead of the things of heaven. He sent his children to the University of Sodom and his wife joined the bridge club and the scripture says, he vexed his righteous soul with the conversation of the wicked. Somebody says he is stilled saved. The Bible says, he was a righteous man. I'll tell you what he lost. He lost his family, his testimony, his friends, his wealth; he lost everything he had because he was out of fellowship with God. He may have been a member of the family of God, perhaps, but out of fellowship with God.

David sent his soldiers into battle, he stayed behind. Because of lust, he took another man's wife, committed adultery. Then he committed murder to try to cover up his sin. In the days that passed, a prophet came to David and said, "David, I want to tell you something that has happened in your kingdom. There is a poor shepherd over here and all he has got to his name is one little lamb. There is a rich shepherd who has many sheep. The rich man has a visitor and he wants to do, as the custom in the east, to provide a feast for his visitor and so he does not go to his flock, but he goes to the poor man's who has one sheep. He steals that one little lamb and brought it back, slayed it and fed it to his visitor. What do you think of that David? David got hot under the collar and said it would never happen in his kingdom. You tell me who it is, David said and I'll see that the man dies. The prophet said, "David, you are the man. You are the one. A little child was born from that relationship and it got sick. It got sick unto death. Like any father, he was wrapped up in that child and he lay on his face before God praying as he watched his child gasp for his last breath. He prayed to God to spare that child of his, saying all the time that if I regard iniquity in my heart, God does not hear me.

It is a dangerous thing to be out of fellowship with God. I would hate for something to happen to my family and they go to the hospital and the doctors and nurses are doing all medical science can do and me out of fellowship with God. Not being able to get in touch with the great physician. I want to close with the parable about the prodigal son. It is a story of a Christian out of fellowship with God. There is also the parable of the prodigal pig. Did you know there was a prodigal pig? II Peter 2:20-22 tell you about the prodigal pig. " For if after they have escaped the pollutions of the world through the knowledge of the Lord and Savior Jesus Christ, they are again entangled therein, and overcome, the latter end is worse with them than the beginning. For it had been better for them not to have known the way of righteousness, than, after they have known it, to turn from the holy commandment delivered unto them. But it is happened unto them according to the true proverb, the dog is turned to his own vomit again; and the sow that was washed to her wallowing in the mire." The prodigal son got up and out of the pig pen and went home and the pig went with him. The pig decided to get washed up. So he went home with the prodigal son. The son got to his father's house and there was a great rejoicing and nothing but happiness. You know the story. In a day or two the pig came to the prodigal son and said, I want to go home. What's the matter? I don't like sleeping on clean sheets. I don't like this food they prepare. I like to put my foot on it and stick my head in it when I eat. I'm going home to my father. And straightway the prodigal pig went back to his house. When he was a far off his father saw him, he just grunted and turned over. The pig jumped head and ears into the wallowing mire of the hog pen.

One of these days, if you are a child of God, you are going to the father's house. One of these days if you are a pig you are going to the Father's house. To be in the family of God; to be in fellowship with God is God's goal for us. Not to just be saved, but to be in fellowship with him.

Are you a member of the family of God today? Can you say God is mine and I belong to him? He is my Savior, he saved me. Can you say I have fellowship with him? I don't know your needs, I only know mine. My greatest need is to have greater fellowship with God. I pray today that the Holy Spirit would speak to your heart. If you are not a member of the family of God, I pray that you become one by experiencing the new birth. If you are a member of the family of God, but out of fellowship with God, it is a dangerous thing. I pray that you will go to the Father's house.

Prayer: Our heavenly Father we thank you for this day and this another opportunity to share a portion of thy word. Father, we pray that as we read the word and listen that the Holy Spirit will speak to our hearts. Father, we know that all of us have spiritual needs. All of us are plagued with the same temptations, the same doubt, and by the same failure. Father, I pray you will help this preacher and every member of this congregation to experience the joy of not only being a member of the family of God but the joy that comes by being in fellowship not only with the Father but with every member of that family. If there are those who have never experienced the new birth; they have never said God be merciful to me a sinner, I pray that today may be the day they receive Christ as their personal Savior. For that Christian, because of sin, indifference or because of unconcern just some way, somehow begin to lose their fellowship with God might today experience the joy of the Father's house. Meet our needs and we will praise you for what you do for us in the precious and holy name of Jesus. Amen.

7

The Second Mile

Matthew 5:41

There is an innocent little sentence in verse 41. It is a sentence that we rationalize and spiritualize and say well isn't that a sweet verse. In that one little verse it reads like this: "And whosoever shall compel thee to go a mile, go with him twain." In that verse of scripture there is enough dynamite to change the world. It is that principle that we overlook and turn aside from, but in this verse Jesus Christ our Lord and Master is teaching us one of the principles of abundant living. There is a difference in living and abundant living. Jesus said, I am come that ye may have life and that ye may have it more abundantly. He meant your life will be more than just living. You have heard me say that there are a lot of folks just walking around to save funeral expenses. They have been dead for a long time, but they are just walking around. Jesus is teaching us that there is a kind of life that is different from the life the world gives and there is a principle involved which, if we accept, would cause us to live abundant lives. I want to have an abundant life; I want to have an exciting life. I want to be able to live differently than the world lives.

Most of us want to have that kind of life, but when Jesus sits down and simply tells us something simple to do we are like Naaman, we refuse to do it. If a man compels thee to go a mile, go with him twain. A Sunday school teacher was giving out this verse for memory and she repeated it several times. She asked her students to memorize the verse and have it ready for next Sunday. The next Sunday, she asked if anyone had the verse memorized. After some hesitation, one fellow raised his hand

and said he could say it. She told him to go ahead. He stood up and said 'and whosoever shall compel thee to go a mile, go with him by train.'

I would like to share with you the background of this verse, which makes it all open up to us. Whenever the Roman Empire captured a city or town, they always took that Roman yoke – the yoke that was put on oxen. They would put this yoke usually at the gate of the city and would make those leaving walk under the yoke. Many times they would make the citizens. It was a permanent thing and every day when they would go to and from their house they had to pass under the Roman yoke. It symbolized their obedience belonged to the Roman Empire. They were in control of the lives of the people they captured. It was another part of that law that if a Roman soldier was going through the countryside carrying his pack and met a young Jewish boy or any Jewish person, the Roman solder could compel them to carry his pack. If he was just walking along and saw someone working, he would say I'm tired, take my pack. The Roman Empire had stipulated that only a mile could be required. So every Jewish boy would go outside their front door and mark off a mile in each direction and would drive a peg in the ground. They could not require anyone to go further than a mile. Each one made sure they knew exactly to the inch how much a mile was and drove a stake in the ground and that was as far as they would go. When a Roman soldier would come by and say, I'm tired, take my pack the boy would get up and when he got to that peg, he would slam the pack down because he knew he was not required to go any further.

With that in mind, let us think about the scene when Jesus Christ is teaching and all the people are gathered around him. He says to them, one sentence, that upsets them more than anything that Jesus has said to them during his ministry. He says to them, 'Whosoever compels thee to go a mile, go with him two.' The people cannot believe their ears. They nudge one another; they say can you believe what he is saying. The most obnoxious thing in the world for us to have to do is to carry a Roman pack for a mile and he is telling us to carry it two. Does he not know what he is saying? It is the most humiliating; the most chafing; the most ridiculous and most obnoxious thing we have been required to do. They punch one another and in their astonishment they say, did you hear what he said. Surely he doesn't not mean for us to do that. But Jesus was using the most obnoxious rule to teach a principle of abundant living. This was what he was preaching in the Sermon on the Mount. Everything Jesus taught was the opposite of what men naturally do. Did you ever notice that whatever Jesus teaches us to live the Christian life it is the opposite of what we would naturally do. A lot of times, in counseling, I ask the question, what would like to do in this situation? They tell me and then I say do the opposite. That is what Paul meant, I think, when he said he had become a fool for Christ sake. A fool does the opposite of what you expect him to do.

What was Jesus teaching when he said, when someone compels thee to go a mile, go with him two? Now Jesus was not speaking literally of going two miles, but he was simply saying to us as Christians that whenever or wherever you are in life, whether at home, office or church, always be willing as a Christian to do more than you are expected to do. He was saying do more than someone requires you to do. Do more than what is just expected of us. Now I want to show you how that can work and how beautiful it is when we put it into practice.

Here is a young Jewish man and he is out in the garden chopping out his beans and a Roman soldier comes by and says, I'm tired, come here and take my pack. The man takes his hoe slams it down on the ground and he drags his feet and slowly climbs the fence. He has got lightening in his eyes and he goes out to where the soldier is and picks up the pack and half dragging, half lifting he gets the pack to the mile peg and slams it down and says, 'if I ever get in control, of the Jewish nation or get to be in control of the Roman Empire, I'll make you carry a ton ten miles'. He goes back to his garden, picks up the hoe and breaks it against the tree and goes home and takes it out on his wife and children.

Now let's take a man who has learned the principle of going the second mile. He is in the garden working, the Roman soldier comes by and says take my pack. The Jewish man jumps over the fence with a smile on his face, picks it up and swings it over his shoulder and begins to march down the road and he gets in conversation with the Roman Soldier. He asked the soldier to tell him about Rome. They begin to talk and when they get to the mile peg he just keeps walking and talking. The soldier says, you have passed the mile stone, the young man says I know but let's just walk along a little bit further. I enjoy talking to you and he walks to the edge of the city and puts the pack down and the Roman soldier takes his hand out of the glove and puts it out and says you have been a friend to me today and I'll think differently about your nation from now on than I have every thought before. And if you every need a friend in the Roman army, you come to me. He goes back to the garden and does two hours work in an hour's time and goes home whistling and his wife comes out and says I know what you have been doing today – you went the second mile, you are always sweeter when you do that.

Let's put the principle to work in our own families. Jesus said do a little more than is expected. When we do more than is expected of us or go the second mile it always leads to happiness in the hearts of those who walk it. The second thing I want us to notice about the second mile is that it lightens life's burdens. My concern is with the home – my concern is with the relationship with husbands and wives in our church family. My concern is that we build the church around the needs of family and not family around the needs of the church. That is what we do by teaching the principles of living. We need to have happy homes. We need to have homes where there is loving leadership on the part of the husband and a loving and willing submission on the part of the wife and obedience on the part of the children. Our nation depends upon that kind of relationship in our homes.

Let's use the second mile principle in our homes. You get up and eat breakfast and begin getting ready for work. Your wife is washing the breakfast dishes and you say to your wife, honey there is a button missing off my shirt, would you mind sewing it on for me. The wife is silent for a moment and finally she slams the dishcloth down in the water and she says, your buttons come off at the most inopportune times. Why didn't you tell me last night that the button was off? So she picks up the shirt and she begins to sew and is fussing all the time she is doing it. When she is finished, she throws it across the chair and goes back to washing dishes. Along about the last of the week she goes to her husband and says, honey, my budget is spent the money you gave me is all gone and I need about ten more dollars to make it. He says, I don't know what you do with the money, I give you enough to run the house and I just don't know what you are doing with it.

Now see it by going the second mile. Husband gets up and says honey I have a button missing. Can you sew it on for me? She smiles and says I just love to sew on buttons for you. I had hoped all night that you would have a button missing so I could sew it on for you this morning. She sews it on and instead of throwing it across the chair she holds it for him to put on and when he puts it on, she short of hugs him a little bit. He goes off to work convinced he has the greatest wife that ever lived. The end of the week comes and she says the budget is spent and she needs ten more dollars. He responds by saying, I don't know how you stretch money as far as you do, here is twenty. That is the principle of going the second mile.

What a difference it would make in our lives if that were the kind of atmosphere we had in our homes. Children would grow up in the atmosphere of love and joy, what a difference that would make in our world, if we were just willing to go that second mile.

And finally, let me say that God went the second mile. Jesus never gave us a commandment that he himself did not live by. God created the heavens and earth, he saw that it was good and God gave every convenience for man. God gave everything we needed. God put us in a paradise where every need would be met godly like and that every desire of the flesh could be fulfilled righteously and God provided for mankind all that mankind needed but man turned away from God choosing rather to go his own way. And through that, man fell in sin and his life became ruined and he became estranged from God through sin and a broken fellowship and relationship. After God had done all of that for man and man turned away – God was willing to go the second mile – God was willing to say to us, I'll give you a second chance. God is forever, the God of second chance. God said I will not quit by doing what is required of me, but I'll do more. I'll do more than was ever expected of me to do. I'll send my Son to be the sacrifice of sin. That whosoever believeth in Him, should not perish but have everlasting life. And God so loved the world that he gave his only begotten Son. Jesus went to the cross of his own will. He says no man takes my life from me; I have the power to lay it down. I have the power to take it up; no man takes it from me. Willingly he gave his life on Calvary. He didn't have to do it. It was just enough for Jesus to come and teach us the Sermon on the Mount and teach us how to live. That's all that could have been expected of Jesus. Surely no one could have required him to do more than that, but he went the second mile. He became obedient unto the father even unto the death of the cross and he took upon himself the form of man and being found in the form of man he became sin for us. He who knew no sin became sin for us that we might become the righteousness of God in him.

Jesus went to Calvary and when they laid him down on the cruel cross and drove the nails through his hands and feet, what was expected of a man in that position? Surely he could curse his enemies, surely he could fight against the cross, and surely he could blaspheme and rebuke them for doing what they were doing. He was innocent! Instead he did more than what was expected and he prayed, 'Father forgive them for they know not what they do'. Yes, God went the second mile. Jesus Christ went the second mile and he taught us that if you want to have abundant life then go the second mile. Be willing to do more than is expected of you; be willing to do more than is required of you. Every time a sinner comes to know Christ as their personal Savior, that prayer that Jesus prayed on the cross is being answered. Father forgive them for they know not what they do. Every time a seeking soul comes and says what must I do to be saved and find themselves at the foot of the cross – that prayer of Jesus is ever ascending into Heaven – Father, forgive; Father, forgive. The father looks down and in mercy and in grace he forgives us our sin because of Jesus and his willingness to go that second mile.

Put the principle of the second mile to work in your home and see what a difference it will make. Let's put the principle of going the second mile into our church and see what a difference it will make. Put it to work where you work. Instead of doing as little as you can for what someone pays you, try to do more. See what a difference it will make in your relationship to your employer. Jesus was not just filling up space, he was giving us a principle of abundant living.

God went the second mile. He not only did what we would expect him to do, but he went more than that. He did more than we could have ever hoped and prayed for by sending his Son to die for us. Jesus was forever walking the second mile. He has not asked us to do anything that he himself didn't do and prove to us on Calvary's cross.

Prayer: Our Father we thank you today for the love that was made manifest to us on Calvary. When you so loved the world that you gave your only begotten Son, that whosoever believeth in him should not perish but have everlasting life. We thank you for the love that he manifest for no greater love hath no man that to lay down his life for a friend. He was going the second mile, not out of requirement, but out of love for us. While we were yet sinners, Christ died for us. Father, I pray that if there is one who has not received you as their personal Savior that will be the time they surrender their hearts to him. For that Christian who needs to rededicate their life to the Lord of the second mile, I trust they will come to you. Whatever the need, I trust you will meet them now. In the name of Jesus and for his sake, I pray. Amen.

8

The Second Coming of Christ

Hebrews 10:37

Hebrews 10:37 says, "For yet a little while, and he that shall come will come, and will not tarry." The word of God rings out, with the truth of the sure and certain fact, that Jesus is coming again. It also rings out the truth that his coming may be at any moment. Sometimes we have problems getting that into our thinking since it has been so many years since the scriptures were written and since they promised an almost immediate return of the Lord. We get our eyes off of that and we suffer because of it. The truth of the matter is the Lord may come at any moment. The Bible is filled with that kind of promise. We believe and have always believed the coming of the Lord is near. When we say the Lord's coming is near doesn't mean he is coming tomorrow or we believe he is coming today. But we do believe he could come today, tomorrow or tonight. He may come while I'm in the middle of this message. He may come tonight while you are lying in bed. He could come at any moment. If that truth gripped our hearts it would have a fantastic effect on the way we live. If all of us really believed that Jesus could come at any moment it would make a difference in the way we live our lives. We would turn loose of the world. We would loosen our hold on things so mighty important to us and we would give our best to the Lord.

I do not know when Jesus is coming again. Jesus himself said he did not know and that only his Father knew. The angels in heaven do not know. I suppose we will have to look at it this way; the Lord knew what he was doing when he hid from us the truth of when the Lord would come. If we knew when the Lord was coming, it would make a big difference, wouldn't it? It would not make a difference for the better. It would make a difference for the worse. If we knew that the Lord was coming back in January of a certain year, isn't it a fact that most of the people in this world would wait until December to make a commitment to Jesus Christ? We do not know when he is coming. The very fact that we do not know when he is coming has an effect on the way we live.

We do not want to be caught unclean or in places we ought not to be. Therefore, it dictates the way we live. Suppose a mother would tell a little girl when she left to go to the store, I've put a new dress on you, now if you will keep that dress clean until I get back, I'll bring you a reward. The little girl wanted that reward and so she remained clean and she received the reward. Suppose, when I was small my mother told me the same thing. I have put you in new overalls and I am going out for a while and return at 5 o'clock and if you have kept those overalls clean, I'll give you a reward. I would take the overalls off, get as filthy as possible and at 4:30 I would start to cleanup and put on the new overalls, wouldn't you? That is exactly what I would do and I think that is the thinking of a lot of people concerning the coming of Jesus Christ. If you knew he was coming next month, you would be trying to make a commitment to God right now.

There are two stages to the coming of the Lord. First, he will come in the air and then he will come to the earth with his saints. The first time he comes he will come for his own and the second time he comes he will come with his own to the earth. Let's go back to some things concerning the Lord's return. The fact is it could be at any moment. I think Matthew 24: 42 – 44 will be a blessing to you. I want to try to reiterate the scripture that has to do with the eminent return of the Lord. Matthew 24:42-44 says, "Watch therefore: for ye know not what hour your Lord doth come. But know this that if the good man of the house had known in what watch the thief would come, he would have watched, and would not have suffered his house to be broken up. Therefore be ye also ready: for in such an hour as ye think not the Son of man cometh."

So we need to watch and wait because we do not know when he is coming. The scripture said it could be at any moment. He illustrated that fact by giving a story of a ruler who had two servants. The ruler took a trip into another country and left those two servants at home to look after his interests while he was gone. The scripture says that while he was away from his estate, one of the servants was faithful to his master. He looked after those things which belonged to the master. He minded his master's business because he did not know when the master would return. Because this servant loved his master, he simply went about the master's business being faithful to that which has been given him to do in his master's absence. The other servant, according to scripture, was unfaithful and the very fact that the master was away, gave him the opportunity for riotous behavior and drunkenness. When the master returned he gave to that good servant a reward and rebuked the unfaithful one. The reason the unfaithful one was not faithful to God was he said with his own mouth, "My master delayeth his coming". In other words, I know he won't come tomorrow, so I'll get drunk tomorrow. I know he won't come tonight, so I won't mind the master's business, I'll have a party tonight. In the midst of the servant saying the master delays his coming, the master suddenly appeared and caught him in a drunken condition. He said to himself, I have plenty of time. You and I do not know when the Lord cometh. Jesus himself said, "therefore watch and be ye ready for you know not what hour the son of man cometh. And he adds this, "the hour you think not the Lord returneth."

Matthew 25: 1 – 13 reads, "Then shall the kingdom of heaven be likened unto ten virgins, which took their lamps, and went forth to meet the bridegroom. And five of them were wise, and five were foolish. They that were foolish took their lamps, and took no oil with them: But the wise took oil in their vessels with their lamps. While the bridegroom tarried, they all slumbered and slept. And at midnight there was a cry made, Behold, the bridegroom cometh; go ye out to meet him. Then all those virgins arose, and trimmed their lamps. And the foolish said unto the wise, give us of your oil; for our lamps are gone out. Bur the wise answered, saying, not so; lest there be not enough for us and you: but go ye rather to them that sell, and buy for yourselves. And while they went to buy, the bridegroom came; and they that were ready went in with him to the marriage: and the door was shut. Afterward came also the other virgins, saying, Lord, Lord, open us. But he answered and said, Verily I say unto you, I know you not. Watch therefore, for ye know neither the day nor the hour wherein the Son of man cometh." The Lord Jesus Christ is pictured as the bridegroom and you and I are to wait for him that we may take part in the great marriage between the bridegroom and his bride, which is the church. The scripture, in this parable, said that there were those who were wise. They had their lamps filled with oil and they were prepared and waiting and watching for the Lord to come. Five of them had their lamps but no oil. And suddenly without any kind of warning the cry went up, the bridegroom is here and they had no oil for their lamps. While some of them were faithful, they were found ready and they entered into blessings of God the other five were foolish and they missed the blessings of God. That's telling us, I believe, that not all of those who profess to be Christians are Christians. The ten of them were all together and all of them were acting the same. You couldn't tell the difference in them. All of them were in the same assembly, they looked alike, they acted alike but some of them had empty lamps. I believe that is a perfect illustration of those of our congregations across the lands that have made an empty profession.

How do you know whether or not your profession is empty? Well, the oil, in the scripture is always pictured as the Holy Spirit. If you do not have the witness of the Holy Spirit, if you do not have communion with the Holy Spirit and if the Holy Spirit is not real to you then you are not His. We must have that fellowship with the Holy Spirit. The scripture says that while they slept the bridegroom came. I wonder if the devil has not lured many of us to sleep. I wonder if maybe through luring the preachers away from preaching concerning the second coming of the Lord Jesus Christ if maybe we have not been lured to sleep and in the hour we think not the Lord will suddenly appear and catch many of us not ready for his coming.

Mark 13: 35 – 37 says, "Watch ye therefore: for ye know not when the master of the house cometh, at even, or at midnight, or at the cockcrowing, or in the morning: Lest coming suddenly he find you sleeping. And what I say unto you I say unto you all, Watch." And Luke 12: 35-37 reads, "Let your loins be girded about, and your lights burning; and ye yourselves like unto men that wait for their lord, when he will return from the wedding; that when he cometh and knocketh, they may open unto him immediately. Blessed are those servants, whom the lord when he cometh shall find watching: verily I say unto, that he shall gird himself, and make them to sit down to meat, and will come forth and serve them". The same warning over and over again watch and be ye ready for ye know not when the Lord cometh. In Luke 17: 30-36, "Even thus shall it be in the day when the Son of man is revealed. In that day, he which shall be upon the housetop and his stuff in the house, let him not come down to take it away: and he that is in the field, let him likewise not return back. Remember Lot's wife. Whosoever shall seek to save his life shall lose it; and whosoever shall lose his life shall preserve it. I tell you, in that night there shall be two men in one bed; the one shall be taken, and the other shall be left. Two women shall be grinding together; the one shall be taken and the other left. Two men shall be in the field; the one shall be taken, and the other left.

I want you to know that there is the scientific accuracy of the creation of the world in these verses. It wasn't until just a short time ago that scientist discovered, over a few hundred years, that the world was round. They had believed it was flat. This verse of scripture declares that the world was round 1900 years ago or more when it was written. How can the Lord come when it is night and yet come while it is yet day? Very simply, the earth is round. It will always be night somewhere when it's day somewhere else. When the Lord comes it will be night time in one part of the country and daytime in the other. There will be those sleeping and there will be those working. Even the scientific accuracy of the world is proclaimed in this passage of scripture.

The apostle in the book of Romans chapter 13 verses 11 and 12 said, " And that, knowing the time, that now it is high time to awake out of sleep: for now is our salvation nearer than when we believed. The night if far spent, the day is at hand: let us therefore cast off the works of darkness, and let us put on the armour of light". What is the kind of salvation Paul is talking about? He is not talking about the salvation of the soul here. He is talking about the salvation of the body that will take place when the Lord comes again. When your body shall be resurrected and you shall be completely redeemed and your salvation will be total in that your body shall be changed and your soul changed with your body. The scripture says we will be like him. In Romans 16: 20, "And the God of peace shall bruise Satan under your feet shortly. The grace of our Lord Jesus Christ be with you. Amen". We know that the Lord hath not bruised Satan as he will when he returns. The devil has a free reign now. The devil is in control of many peoples' lives. He is the prince of god of the world. But in the day when the Lord comes, Christ shall finally crush his head and Satan will no longer be able to tempt us.

In 1 Corinthians 1:7 Paul reminds the Corinthians, "So that ye come behind in no gift; waiting for the coming of our Lord Jesus Christ". Paul even says keep your life in good shape. Let there be nothing that you have not done that needs to be done. Don't get behind in your offering, don't get behind in your praying, don't get behind in your Bible reading; don't get behind in anything in your life because you are waiting for the coming of the Lord Jesus

Christ. He says see that you get behind in nothing waiting for the coming of Christ.

In Hebrews 10:25, the scripture says, "Not forsaking the assembling of ourselves together, as the manner of some is: but exhorting one another: and so much the more, as ye see the day approaching." He is referring to faithful church attendance. Why should we be faithful to church attendance other than it's a place to go to worship. It is a place to hear from the Word of God. Another reason is the Lord may come at any moment. Do not forsake the assembling of yourselves the much more as you see the day approaching and exhort one another because as the days come close to the coming you are going to need all the strength and fellowship that you can get from one another.

James 5 talks about the coming of the Lord being near. Now what do we get from the fact that the Lord says, I am going to come and it may be at any moment? I may come suddenly and in fact, I will come in the very hour that you expect not. There is some blessings to come from that kind of hope. I don't know of a better incentive to right living than that fact. The scripture says those who have that hope purify themselves. In other words, if I believe the Lord is coming and believe that he can come at any moment, then I purify my life. It is an incentive for me to live right. It is a good motive for me that the Lord might come at any moment. I don't want to be ashamed at the Lord's coming.

Not only does that hope make us live better, but that hope causes us to have comfort. Paul, in the book of Thessalonians said to those believers who had lost loved ones; don't be concerned about those who died in the Lord because Jesus is coming again and those who have died already will not have missed anything. For when the Lord comes, those who have died already will be the first to be resurrected. So there is comfort in that statement.

It also produces patience. James said, be patient until the coming of the Lord. Now they were being oppressed, mistreated and executed as Christians and James says to them, "He is coming again and he is going to bring a reward with him and he will lift your burdens and will take you out of the oppression, so be ye patient until the coming of the Lord." It is a cure for worry. Philippians 4 tells us the Lord is at hand. Be careful for nothing, be anxious for nothing for when the Lord comes he is going to straighten everything out. The conditions in this world are rotten. When the Lord comes personally, nationally and every other way he will straighten them out and we will go home to be with him in Paradise.

The scripture we read about the Lord coming and he might come at any moment has been laughed at by scoffers who say, yes he promised to come but ever since our fathers fell asleep all things continue as they were. Where is the promise of His coming? Why has He postponed His coming? Why does He tarry his coming? Why does this old sinful world in which we live go on and on? Why doesn't God take his blood washed saints out of this world? Well, that is one of the questions we don't know the answer to because we look through the glass darkly, but there is a clue. While the Lord tarries the first thing that happens in my mind and in your mind is we begin to realize how desperately in need this world is for a leader. How desperately in need we are of someone who is capable of straightening out the things that need to be straightened out. So as the Lord tarries we begin to lose our faith in ourselves to be able to do things the way we want them. We begin to lose faith, in the fact, that no man can do it, so we look for the coming of the Lord. When he shall come, he will be the perfect leader.

Also the Lord displeases longsuffering. Jesus said come unto me and I will give you rest. Over and over he is inviting people to come. But what are men doing? Are they coming to him? Not many. Are they turning to God in any kind of large numbers? No. In fact, the world is getting wicked and all of that proves God is longsuffering. God is patient. It means you cannot exhaust the love of God in a few years. But God's love is the kind of love you and I cannot understand. You know I would have gotten on my nerves a long time ago. I would have been fed up with me already. But God is longsuffering and patient. The fact that he tarries His coming or that He is trying now only proves to us that God's love cannot be explained.

There was a man who was preaching one time and an atheist was in the crowd who began to heckle him. The heckler ran up to the preacher and said if there is a God I pray that he would strike me dead at this moment. He said I do not believe there is a God and if there is let him strike me dead. He stood there for a second or two and nothing happened and he laughed and said you see there is no God. The preacher said, Sir, do you think the God who so loved the world that he gave his only begotten Son, do you believe the Lord of glory who was willing to die on the cross of Calvary do you believe that you can exhaust that kind of love in 30 seconds? You cannot exhaust God's love by shaking your fist in his face. You cannot exhaust his love by cursing him. He loves you in spite of all that. His longsuffering is almost unexplainable.

Maybe he is tarrying because he wants to test the faith of his children. God has always dealt like that. Why did Abraham have to wait so long for Isaac? Why did God promise Abraham a son and then wait until Abraham was 99 years old before he gave him that son? Why so long? Did he not teach Abraham, during that time, to have confidence in him? Did he not test Abraham's faith? Why did Israel have to remain in Egypt so long in bondage? Why did generation after generation have to die in slavery? Was he not teaching them to trust him and to have confidence in him? Why did it take so long from the promise of His first coming until He was actually born in Bethlehem? Why did it take so long for that to happen? And why has it taken so long since prophets, apostles and disciples for him to come again? It has been so long because He is teaching and preparing us. Why has He been so long in the Father's house? He is testing and building a people to have confidence in him.

The scoffers say where is the promise of his coming? There is a reason for his delay. The question is are you ready for his coming? Do you really believe that he is coming? Do you believe he could come tonight and if you do are you ready for him to come? Are you ready for the Lord? The scripture says, seeing that we have that hope and every man that has that hope purifieth himself. Seeing that the Lord come at any moment what kind of lives ought we to be living?

Do you need to make a change in your life? In face of the fact that he could come in the next 30 minutes or next week or next month would your life need to make any changes?

Prayer: Our heavenly Father we thank you for your great love to us. We thank you that while we were astray going our own way and while we were yet sinners you sent your Son to come into the world to die for us. Because of that death on the cross, we have access to the throne of God. Father, we thank you for all the possibilities involved in salvation. We thank you for the new creature, the new creation that is possible through coming to the Lord Jesus Christ. We thank you for your promise of coming again. We realize from time to time we forget that great promise and we live as though you could not come at any moment. We know when we study the scripture that your coming could be at any moment. Help us to let that truth get down into our very being. Help us to be gripped by the fact that you could come at any time and seeing that help us to change our lives. Father we pray that most of all, during this time we wait for your returning that we would heed your command to occupy till you come. Help us to be concerned for lost souls and to weep over those who are lost. May we witness to those who need the Lord and cooperate with the ministry of the church in reaching lost souls. Our prayer is that you not come and catch us unprepared. Help us to watch and be ready and have many with us when you return. I pray that if there is one who is not ready for the sudden return of the Lord that the Holy Spirit will speak to that heart. I pray if there is a Christian who needs to get some things straightened out in their lives waiting for the Lord that they will do so now. If there is one who does not know you as their personal Savior, I pray that they will accept you today. Have your own way in our hearts and we will praise you for all that is done. In Jesus' name. Amen

9

The Lost Boy

Luke 15:11-24

In Luke 15 there are the parables of the lost coin and the lost sheep. There is also a story of the lost boy. I am sure you have probably heard the story of the prodigal more times than any other Bible story. I would like to spend time refreshing our minds about what the prodigal son is teaching.

I think it probably tells us more or can be used in more ways to teach Biblical truths than any other story in the Bible. We have, for example, the story of the elder brother. Most people overlook the elder brother. There is a series of sermons that could be preached and a series of lessons that could be taught on the attitude of the elder brother. There is certainly a lot of preaching about the father figure and that is what the story is about - the father and not the son. There is a great deal of preaching and teaching that can be done about the prodigal son himself: how he became the prodigal son. We have the story of sin, the story of salvation and the story of winning someone to Christ. It is one of the richest stories in the Bible. It is just filled with interpretations and there are three things I want to notice.

Luke 15:11-24 "And he said, a certain man had two sons: and the younger of them said to his father, Father, give me the portion of goods that falleth to me. And he divided unto them his living. And not many days after the younger son gathered all together, and took his journey into a far country, and there wasted his substance with riotous living. And when he had spent all, there arose a mighty famine in that land; and he began to be in want. And he went and joined himself to a citizen of that country; and he sent him into his fields to feed swine. And he would fain have filled his belly with the husks that the swine did eat: and no man gave unto him. And when he came to himself, he said, How many hired servants of my fathers have bread enough and to spare, and I perish with hunger! I will arise and go to my father, and will say unto him, Father, I have sinned against heaven, and before thee. And am no more worthy to be called thy son: make me as one of thy hired servants. And he arose, and came to his father. But when he was yet a great way off, his father saw him, and had compassion, and ran, and fell on his neck, and kissed him. And the son said unto him, Father, I have sinned against heaven, and in thy sight, and am no more worthy to be called thy son. But the father said to his servants, Bring forth the best robe, and put it on him; and put a ring on his hand, and shoes on his feet: And bring hither the fatted calf, and kill it; and let us eat, and be merry: For this my son was dead, and is alive again; he was lost, and is found. And they began to be merry".

I want us to notice three things about the story of the prodigal son. I want us to, first of all, notice the power of sin. We usually talk about the father's compassion and so forth. I want us to notice the power of sin as it is pictured in this story. The boy is at home and I really relate to this prodigal son. I have been in his shoes more times than a few. I've run away from home several times, not lately, but when I was a boy. Back in my younger days, boys ran away from home. You put your lunch in a handkerchief and put it over your back and ran away from home. Now when a kid wants to run away from home, he calls his father and says call me a cab, I'm going to leave home. Things have changed since my day of running away. I had an elder brother who was three years older than I was and I tried my best to kill him before I got to the age of eighteen. He and I fought day and night, so I know what it is like to have an elder brother, exactly like this one. My elder brother fits the picture of this elder brother perfectly. All Ralph ever wanted to do was work. There is something wrong with a man like that. He could never understand my foolishness. He never did appreciate it and just as soon as Dad would turn his back, I would do something and then Ralph would set upon me and there would be a ruckus.

I know what the prodigal son was feeling in his heart. He was at home and dissatisfied. He didn't like restraints, I suppose, his father had placed upon him. He certainly didn't like the self-righteousness of his elder brother. He began to dream about what was on the other side of the fence, so to speak. He began to make plans. I am sure all of you young people have said, if I ever get to the age of eighteen, I'm not staying home any longer. I'll not listen to mom and dad anymore. I'll be my own boss and hit the trail. Well, it is not nearly as much fun as you think. But the prodigal son began to dream. He began to dream perhaps about the bright lights and all the fun he heard folks were having who lived in the big city. He begins to make his plans for the day in which he could leave home and he even secured his part of the inheritance. His father was not yet dead, but he persuaded his father to go ahead and divide the inheritance and give him his share in advance.

With a mind full of dreams and a pocket full of money and probably riding a big fine horse, this young boy begins to make his journey into the far country. I am sure he had a fun time because the scripture says he wasted his substance with riotous living. He enjoyed every experience that he ever dreamed about. He had all the friends you could possibly want, he had money and was having himself a real good time. Suddenly things begin to change. He was a lot like I am, he didn't know how to balance his checkbook and when you haven't got anything to balance it with it is even more difficult. He didn't realize it, but his money began to slip away faster than he had planned. The first thing you know he didn't have any money. Maybe you have experienced when you run out of money you run out of friends. He noticed he couldn't buy what he use to buy and he couldn't go to a friend's house like he use to before because his friends were turning their backs on him. He was in dire need all of the sudden.

How many of you know that is a picture of a sinner? This is the perfect picture of every one of us when we were yet without Christ. We do not want to be restrained by the Ten Commandments. We do not want to be restrained by the laws of God and we feel the call of sin and the far country. There is the lust of the flesh, physical pull of the flesh. There is the emotional and intellectual and it's just pulling upon us and we don't want to be constrained by any laws, especially the laws of God. The laws of mom and dad are bad enough. But to buckle down to the laws of God is even worse. So we enter into sin. And we enjoy it for a season. Somebody said one time, Preacher, I heard a preacher one time talk about sin and how miserable it was and I could never reconcile that statement. If it was so miserable why do so many folks do it? The reason is it is pleasurable. There is pleasure in sin and if there weren't people wouldn't commit sin. There is pleasure in sin at least for a season.

Then the misery comes. The unhappiness comes and we find ourselves with misery and unhappiness as our portion. If a man lives in sin, he pays the price for sin. Folks say people can do all kinds of things and God doesn't strike them down. Well, anytime, you commit sin you are going to pay for it. You may pay for it slowly, but you will pay for it. For example, a man begins to drink and God doesn't strike him dead. He continues to drink and God lets him live a prosperous life while all the time his liver is drying up; all the time his ulcers are becoming more infected. God is punishing him through the very action of his physical body to that drink. Man cannot just sin and escape. Outside of the love of God there is nothing as strong as sin. There is nothing as strong as the call of sin. It is terribly powerful. Sin will degrade a man. Sin will take a man who is in high position and pull him down. How many times have we seen this happen? During the Watergate affair there were people who had risen to the top politically and socially. They began to enter into sin and the whole foundation was swept from under them. Sin will take a man that is clean and make him dirty. Sin defeats a man. Sin destroys and if a man holds on to it, it will pull a man into hell. Sin begins in a man's life in a small way. The thief does not begin, most of the time, by stealing ten thousand dollars. There was a story of a man who had served many years in prison because he was a thief. He had become converted and was telling his life's story. They ask him how he began his life of stealing. He began it right in his own church. He began stealing in Sunday school taking little things from the church, things from the Sunday school class. Little by little, he began to become a thief in a bigger and bigger way. Every time he took something his conscience would say to him you ought not to do that.

I baptized a young man in Nashville a number of years ago who was an usher in an Episcopalian church. He and four more fellows took the offering every Sunday morning and he told me they always took out an usher's fee. The four would go back to a room, count the money and take out a certain amount and put it in their pocket. Can you imagine a man walking down the aisle of a church watching folks as they drop their money so as soon as he could get to the back door he would put it in his pocket? Sin always begins in a man's life in a small way. The first time you ever committed sin, your conscience gave you a real lashing. Many of you can remember the first time you felt the pains of conscience. You must have said to yourself, I won't do it anymore, but you found it a little bit easier to do it the next time until finally your conscience no longer condemned you when you sinned. By that time, you were caught in the grip of sin. Sin had you in its net.

In Israel there is 65 miles from the Sea of Galilee to the Dead Sea. The Jordan River comes out of the Sea of Galilee and enters into the Dead Sea 65 miles further down which puts the Jordan River 200 miles long. Only 65 miles from one body of water to another but the river itself is 200 miles long because it is a winding, curving crooked river. The reason was that when it began, the water started running and it would hit a solid place and go somewhere else, hit another solid place and go somewhere else. It just wound its way, the way of least resistance. If there was nothing there to stop it, it kept going, but if it came upon something it would turn and therefore went 200 miles to go 65 miles. That is the way sin begins. We take the way of least resistance.

It is not easy to put up a fight. I am glad I don't have to go through high school again. I'm glad that is all behind me. I'm glad I didn't have sense enough to know what drugs were when I was in school. What I'm saying is we did not have near the temptations and in those days a teacher didn't mind slapping your jaws if you needed it. It is easy to take the way of least resistance. It is easy for a kid in high school to quit fighting. It is easy for them to say why fight all the time, to try and stand for your convictions. It's a lot easier to just do what everybody else is doing. That way you would be accepted by your peers and who wants to be a martyr anyway. So we take the way of least resistance. It is an unusual young person who has the ability and the conviction and courage to stand and fight for what they believe in. When we take the road of least resistance, we are finally caught in the net of sin. That shows us the power of sin has over our lives.

Then we notice, secondly, the poverty of the sinner. Look how poor he became. The scripture says in verse 14-15, and when he had spent all, there arose a might famine in that land; and he began to be in want. And he went and joined himself to a citizen of that country; and he sent him into his fields to feed swine. Can you imagine how degrading that was for that young boy to take a job feeding pigs? He was a Jew. Can you imagine how repulsive it was for him to be around swine? When I was in Israel in 1970, I could not wait until we left Israel and got into Greece so I could get some sausage. Brother, you don't find pork in Israel. It would have been degrading; it would have been the worst possible thing for a young Jew to find himself doing; that of feeding swine.

He not only fed the swine, but he came to the point where he was willing to eat the slop that he was feeding the pigs. Now that's a picture of a sinner. Sinners are poor. They may be rich with physical things but they are just as poor as this boy was. Jesus said, "What shall it profit a man if he gain the whole world and lose his own soul?" What is Christ saying? He is saying that the richest man in the world without Christ is the poorest man that ever lived. If you spend your whole life without Christ, what is your profit? Could you believe with me that the Christian is rich? We may not have a great deal of physical things or material things but the Christian is rich. I have just not come into my inheritance yet, but, it is there for me. I don't have to live and wait till someone else dies to get it. It's mine and it is waiting for me. There is a heavenly home waiting for the Christian. There is a reward awaiting the Christian. The Christian is rich. What does a lost man have waiting for him? Nothing but outer darkness, nothing but despair. The Christian has a place waiting, a place where there is no sickness; where there is a great reunion; where the Savior is waiting to reward him.

Then finally, we have the picture of the Savior. We have the power of sin, the poverty of the sinner then we have a perfect picture of the Savior. The prodigal son came to himself. That is, the light came on, understanding came. He came to himself realizing first that he was hopeless, realizing secondly that he was in a helpless condition and be begins to think about the father's house.

Isn't it strange how we were when we were young? We use to think our parents were stupid. If we could just get away from mom and dad; if we could just leave home how better our life would be. But when we began to get into trouble, isn't it odd that we begin to think about the father's house. Regardless of how we thought our fathers were; regardless of their personality there was just something about the father's house. When I lost my father, it was the strangest feeling. I didn't show my father how much I loved him. Maybe, I didn't know how much I loved him until he died. But brother, when your dad is gone you know that the one person who loved you and the one person you could go to, is gone forever. You don't have him anymore. The one person that you had is dad. And when dad is gone, it is an overwhelming feeling.

The son came to himself and began to think about the father's house and all that was his when he was back home. He may not have liked his dad's personality; he may not have liked his dad's discipline but he began to think about all the good things he had in his father's house. He had a fine horse to ride, good clothes to wear, good food to eat, he had position, he had social standing, and he had blessings untold in his father's house. He began to think on all those things. He begins to think humbly now and decides to go home. He begins to say to himself, if I was back home and if I could just do what the servants in my father's house are doing, I would be well off. At least they have a roof over their head, clothes and food and I don't even have that. He makes up his mind that he is going home. Not only is he going home but he rehearses ahead of time what he is going to say when he gets there. I remember rehearsing many a speech before I went home. I knew exactly what I was going to tell daddy and I would keep going over it in my mind until it sounded good. I had me a good speech. I might sweat and I might twist and turn, but I would tell my daddy the story and look him straight in the eyes. He knew I was lying but it makes you feel so dumb to stand there and tell this elaborate story and see the expression on your father's face. You can tell he didn't believe a word of it. All you can think of the razor strap and you just wish you had gone home and said Dad, I'm guilty, pour it on.

The prodigal son said he was going home and tell his father he was a sinner. The boy left riding the finest horse and wearing the best clothes and he comes back walking on foot, ragged, dirty and hungry with just a little spark of hope. He is going to say to his father I want to come back home. I don't expect to be made a son, just make me a servant, hire me, and put me on the payroll.

I am not worthy to be called a son. He begins this long trip back home and finally gets to the top of the hill and sees a very familiar place. He sees the old home place. He sees a very familiar face, he sees his father. He sees this father running to him. If I were that young boy, I would have said to myself, boy I've had it now. He can't wait to get his hands on me, he's running. He is going to lecture me, he is going to correct me, and he is going to punish me and can't wait to do it. I am willing to endure whatever my father throws at me if he will just take me back.

Finally, the father reaches the son and the father wraps his arms around him and hugs him and begins to kiss him. The son explains that he has sinned and is not worthy to be his son. The father did not even answer him. The father turned to the servants and ordered them to kill the fatted calf. Not only did the father forgive him, he prepared a feast for him. If that is not a true picture of God, I don't know what a picture of God would be. Not only is he willing to forgive us, but he is willing to give us, at the same time, all the good things of life.

When we realize, as this young boy, that we are willing to go back and willing to repent and say to the father, I have sinned, Christ will forgive us. He will bring both the robe of righteousness, the ring of adoption and the sandals of peace and put them on us and kill the fatted calf and the feast begins. Remember the song, O Happy Day that fixed my choice on my Savior and my God.

Do you remember the day you went back to the father's house? Do you remember the tears? Do you remember the joy and peace that came into your heart? Do you remember the assurance? That was a happy day when we went home. There is a spot to me dearer than native vale or mountain, the spot to which affection's tear spring forth from its fountain. Tis not the place where kindred souls abound, though that's almost heaven. But where I first my Savior found and felt my sins forgiven.

Charles Finney tells the story of when he was ministering in Detroit. A man came to him one time and wanted him to go home with him after the service and talk to him about his soul. Charles Finney, like any other preacher, was eager to go. After the service someone called him to the side and told him that the man was a dangerous man. He was one of the most notorious hoodlums in Detroit. He was told it would be dangerous to go to the man's home. But Finney had already committed himself, so he went to this man's home. When he got into the man's home, the man took his pistol out of his pocket and laid it on the table. He said, Preacher, that pistol has killed four men. (People have a way of making a preacher feel right at home) Do you think there is any hope for me? Charles Finney said these words, "The blood of his Son cleanses us from all sin." He said, Preacher, I have spent, in times past, every dime that I have gambling and there have been times that my wife and daughter have actually gone hungry. Do you think there is any hope for me? Charles Finney repeated, "The blood of his Son cleanses us from all sin." He told the preacher that he owned a bar and watched men come into the bar and spend the last cent that they had and their wives would come to me and beg me not to sell their husbands any more booze and I ran them away. Do you think there is any hope for me? Finney again said, the blood of his Son cleanses us from all unrighteousness. The man said, Preacher, if you really believe that I am going to give my heart to the Lord. The next morning this man went and broke up his bar, broke up every gambling device and went to the church and he, his wife and little girl gave their hearts to the Lord and joined the church. He became a dedicated servant of the Lord. Now none of us have been that mean, I don't think. What Jesus Christ did for him he has done for all of us? What he had done for other people he has done for us. The blood of his Son cleanses us from all unrighteousness. Yes, when we sin, Jesus Christ is willing and waiting to rush out. If we, through repentance and faith, will come to him and say, Father against thee and thee only have I sinned. He is willing as this father was to rush out and forgive us.

If you have not accepted Christ as your personal Savior, he's waiting to rush out and wrap you in his arms, if you will only receive him as your Savior.

Prayer: Our heavenly Father, we thank you for thy word. We thank you for the Holy Spirit and for the moments we share together. Father, we pray through the preaching of your word that hearts would be established and be encouraged and those who are not saved would be saved and come to know Christ as their personal Savior. If there is one who needs to feel the father's compassion; perhaps some Christian who has taken their journey into the far county and need to come back home and feel the loving arms of the heavenly, I pray they come. Father, you know the need of every heart and we just leave this invitation to you. We commit to you and ask you to have your way in every heart. We will praise you for what you will do. In the precious name of Jesus. Amen.

10

The Logic of Faith

Mark 11:20-24

Jesus, the day before in this passage, had been walking along and came to a fig tree. He was hungry and went to find figs to eat. The tree had no figs and Jesus cursed the tree and said from hereafter you will not bare any fruit. The disciples heard him. He went into the temple and cast out those who were buying and selling in the temple.

Then in verse 20-24 the scripture says, "And in the morning, as they passed by, they saw the fig tree dried up from the roots. And Peter, calling to remembrance, saith unto him, Master, behold the fig tree which thou cursedst is withered away. And Jesus, answering, saith unto them, Have faith in God. For verily I say unto you, Whosoever shall say unto this mountain, Be thou removed, and be thou cast into the sea; and shall not doubt in his heart, but shall believe that those things which he saith shall come to pass, he shall have whatever he saith. Therefore, I say unto you, whatsoever things ye desire, when ye pray, believe that ye receive them, and ye shall have them." That passage has gotten more people into trouble than it has gotten out of trouble. I have come to realize that this passage of scripture is a very difficult one for the Christian. There are many people that are teaching that you do not have the things you desire; it is your fault because you have not exercised your faith. They teach that God wants no Christian sick, he wants no Christian poor, he wants no Christian to have adversities, and so if you pray and ask God to remove those things from you and believe in your heart that you've got them, you've got them. Now if you pray and don't get it they say you have got it already, but you just haven't claimed it yet. They preach that all you have to do is to just claim that which you ask for and it will be yours because God has already given it to you.

I saw a man one time who believed all that he was taught concerning faith and he prayed and asked God for the desire of his heart. God didn't give it to him and his faith was shipwrecked. He didn't know how to handle it or cope with it. He had been taught all his life that if you believe, and pray God will give you what you ask for and when God didn't do it, he didn't know which way to turn. His whole faith in God was ruined by the one act of God holding back that thing for which he prayed.

Another man said to me one time, Brother, if a man believes in his heart and can go over to this bluff and say, bluff, be removed into the Cumberland River and that bluff would just go right off into the river. My response to him was, what happens when the bluff don't move? What happens when you pray and the mountain does not move? I'll tell you what happens, you send those people back to the Baptist. They don't belong in your outfit. They don't fit in. I want us to teach a little bit and try to learn a little about the logic of faith.

The Christian religion is not nearly as mysterious as some folks would have us believe. The religion of Jesus Christ is intensely practical. It is a logical, reasonable faith. Now some have obscured the real and vital issues of life by speaking on some learned dissertations about some abstract objects. But there are some who have obscured the real issues of life by taking the scriptures and used faith as some kind of magic wand and tried to force from the scriptures those things which the scriptures would not yield and give up. They use faith like a magician uses a magic wand and claim promises. They work themselves up into an emotional mess and they love the Lord with all their heart. Faith is logical. Faith is reasonable and practical. God had to make it that way. Now I know that life is full of glorious moments. There are mountaintop faith experiences in every Christian's life and I thank God for them. But there are a lot of valleys. The Holy Spirit was not given to us that we might live on the mountaintop all the time. Yes, there are mountaintop experiences, but the Holy Spirit was not given to us for a thrill. What really happens in the Christian life is how you walk through the valleys. How your faith is when you are really down in the valley, between the mountaintop experiences. Life is glorious and there are great moments of faith. I believe the word 'life' means exactly to us what the word 'God' means to us.

Faith is not just some important element in the Christian religion, it is the foundation from which Christianity is built. What is faith? I believe that a good definition of faith is the acceptance of testimony. Faith is not twisting God's arm. Faith is not coming to a passage of scriptures which says, and if he will ask whatever he desires God will give it to him, and twisting God's arm around that verse and say God you've got to give it to me because you promised it to me in your word.

Faith is visualizing what God intends to do in any situation that comes into our life. One of the situations might be sickness. There are three kinds of sicknesses in the Bible. There is a sickness unto death; when folks get sick they die. There is a sickness unto glorification. In John the people asked of the blind man, who sinned, him or his parents. Jesus said neither; this man was made this way for the glory of God. God would be glorified through his sickness. So some folks get sick so that God may be glorified through that experience in their life. There is the sickness of chastisement. Paul said, "For this reason, for your misconduct, many of you are sick and some of you are even dead." So what do you do when you are sick? You don't pray for the mountain to be moved. You try to visualize what God is intending to do with your life. He is either going to let you die or he is going to glorify himself through your sickness or he is whipping you, one of the three. So you pray the prayer of faith, visualizing what God intends to do in your life.

Now I know of some marvelous things that have happened through the prayer of faith and sicknesses; and I have witnessed them with my own eyes. I've seen it, but whatever you pray, faith is the accepting of testimony. What testimony are you and I as Christians asked to receive? The testimony that you and I are asked to receive is nothing less than the glorious gospel of Jesus Christ. Is that testimony credible? Can we believe it? I could spend 35-45 minutes telling you why we ought to believe the word of God but I've little sense enough to believe that if you didn't believe in God you wouldn't be here this morning. History says yes we can trust the word of God. The fame, that has lived with the apostles every since those days, says yes. The martyrs, who died for their faith, say yes we can believe that the word of God is credible and we can accept the testimony of the word of God.

Brethren, there is a lot of unbelief among us believers. If we were to accept as readily the testimony of God as we do man, we would grow in our Christian life. If we could believe God as quickly as we believe man. There are folks who believe in the God of creation, the God of Abraham and Moses and God is the eternal now. He is the same yesterday, today and forever. The testimony that you are I are called upon to believe is more real than the testimony which Abraham and Moses were called to believe. You do realize that the testimony that Abraham, Moses and Noah were called to believe were things that said that God had said would happen. They were asked to believe in something that was going to happen. We say we wish we had the faith of those guys. But the testimony that challenges our faith – we are asked to believe things that have already been accomplished. We are not asked to believe something that is yet to come. We base our faith on things that are already accomplished and recorded in the word of God.

Faith is something reasonable and logical. If I do not believe it then I am held accountable to God for being unreasonable. Now let's talk about faith. Logical and reasonable faith does not

IN MY FATHER'S WORDS

demand what God has denied. Brethren, there are some things that are right and there are some things that are wrong. They will always be right and wrong and they never change. Reasonable faith does not demand something that God has denied in his Word. Whatever God says and affirmed and denied must stand, regardless of where you and I stand and what we believe.

For example, God has denied that a man can be saved in sin. Nowhere in the Bible do you find the promise that a man can be saved in sin. You may think that is not a very important subject, but more and more we are finding that people believe that they can live anyway they want to and God will save them. They have no assurance from the Word of God. Logical faith does not demand what God has denied. The scripture says that Jesus came to save from sin, not to save in sin. Folks say, well God loves me the way I am. That is true, God does love you the way you are, but God is not going to leave you the way you are. God is going to change you. God saves from sin not in sin. You would be surprised the wild testimonies we hear of people living in open rebellion against God and claiming to be saved. They have no assurance for it in the Word of God. They certainly do not have any reasonable, logical faith and believe that.

Listen to what Jesus said, "If ye believe not that I am he, ye shall die in your sin". We cannot by the stretch of the imagination force God to say something that he has denied. Folks that have that kind of faith do not have reasonable faith, nor do they have a logical faith. They do not have a faith that is based on the Word of God. The natural laws which we live in are unchangeable, they are immutable. Summer follows spring, fall follows summer and winter followers fall. The seasons are unchangeable. You cannot violate the natural laws of God without paying a penalty for it. In the national laws, you must avoid something and you must do certain things.

For example, a man can cross the ocean as long as he is in a ship. But if a man falls overboard, he cannot wrestle with the billows

SHEILA BOYD COOK   99 of the sea. They will drown him. You can light your home with electricity, but if you come in contact with that force, in your body, it means certain death for you. You see you have to avoid some things and you have to do some things to live in harmony with God's natural laws. God is the author of natural law. God is also the author of spiritual laws. Unless we are in harmony with those laws, we cannot have God's blessings. No logical faith can demand that we can have harmony with God and violate the spiritual laws.

People with say, Preacher, the physical laws are controlled by law and the spiritual laws are controlled by grace. That is exactly right. That is why Jesus came. That was the reason for the atonement and the death on the cross. The law demanded death and Jesus came and stood in our place. The cross of Jesus Christ is a demonstration of God's mercy to us. Now if that is true, if Jesus died for my sins, is it not reasonable to believe that God can and should deny salvation to those who will not accept it. It's logical and practical. If Jesus died for my sin and I do not receive Christ into my heart, then God is reasonable and right to deny me salvation.

The natural law says whatsoever a man sow, that shall he also reap. The spiritual law says that if a man doesn't sow, he doesn't reap. Just as seed has to be placed into the soil in order for there to be reproduction, so does the seed of life which is Jesus Christ have to be planted in the hearts of the soul of man that there be a spiritual harvest and eternal life.

Reasonable faith does not ask that God bless a godless life. Reasonable faith does not demand that God pour out his blessings on a selfish life. Brother, if my aim in life is myself, I have no one to blame if I don't attain. My reward can be nothing beyond my own attainment if that is what I set my sights on. God is under no obligation to bless me if that's what my aim is. People say, I don't know why God's blessings aren't as real to me as they are to someone else. When you invite God out of your life, he accepts that invitation. He withholds his spiritual blessings. Logical faith accepts that.

God denies the riches of his grace to divided life. Right after he got through saving you, whatever you desire just ask for it and you'll have it and the next verse says, 'and when you stand praying, forgive if you have anything against your brother'. If you don't forgive your brother, don't pray. That is what he said. A lot of people think they can hold onto God with one hand and hold onto the pleasures of the world with the other. God says in his Word that our citizenship is in heaven. God says you cannot serve God and man. He also tells us that a house divided against itself cannot stand. We must have a single eye upon him and reasonable faith expects nothing less. Reasonable faith does not demand God bless a divided life.

Logical faith does not demand something God hasn't promised. If we are going to have the promises of God, we have to put ourselves within the promises of God, in order to get it. Someone says, brother, my faith is weak. My faith is just about gone. I ask them why you are having such a struggle with your faith. My loved one died. Let me ask you something has God ever promised anything else? Has God ever made one promise close to anything other than that? Did he promise that our loved one would not die? Does not God say exactly the opposite? Does God not say that all life is like the grass that is cut down and withers away? Does not God's word say that death is a part of God's divine purpose and divine program? I have known people who have lost a loved one and their faith in God was completely shattered. Their faith wasn't based upon the Word of God because God never promised that wouldn't happen to you. God never promised that your husband or child wouldn't die, but God promised the other.

Logical faith does not demand anything else from him. Someone said my faith is failing. Why brother, why don't you have that same faith you had when you first became a Christian. They say, because my burdens are so heavy. Did God promise that you wouldn't have sorrow in life or that you wouldn't have burdens in life? No, but he told you what to do. "Cast your burden upon the Lord and he shall sustain thee for I have overcome the world", Psalms 55:22. Logical faith expects suffering. Logical faith demands sorrow. Reasonable, logical invites adversity. Logical faith accepts bereavement. Logical faith accepts death, not the opposite.

When our missionaries go overseas, God never promised they wouldn't have the diseases and die. I know some missionaries who have gone and been killed by the natives. People say let's not send any more missionaries; it's a waste of life. Christ gave his life for the preaching of the truth. A faith that demands something that God's word has not declared denies the very truth of God's word.

Logical faith does not expect what God has promised except on the conditions of past. Do you think a man can eat without conveying food to his mouth? Do you think a man can walk without using his limbs? Do you think a man can sleep without closing his eyes? Same is true in the spiritual life. If I were to be saved, then I must repent of my sins. I must forsake it and I must turn to God. That's logic; that's what faith teaches. If I would be blessed by the ministrations of the Lord's Day then I must be in the Spirit on the Lord's Day. Reasonable and logic faith does not demand that we have a model departmentalized Sunday school, for example, when the majority of the members do not attend Sunday school. Faith does not demand we have that model Sunday school class. Reasonable faith does not demand we have a healthy budget with money in the bank when members will not support the budget. Logical faith does not demand we have a flourishing prayer meeting when people make no effort to attend. But rather, God bless the faithful few and may their number ever increase.

Reasonable faith does not demand the salvation of your loved one unless you are interested in their salvation and pray to God that they be saved. Reasonable faith does not demand the conversion of our children when parents say they are either too young or they do not demand their attendance in the service. Reasonable faith does not demand knowledge of God's word when the Bible is sitting on the shelf gathering dust. Reasonable faith does not expect unbelievers on the outside to remember the Sabbath day and keep it holy when believers are doing a thousand things to desecrate it. Reasonable faith does not demand an entrance into the marriage supper of the Lamb when there is not oil in the vessel.

Let me make a few positive statements. If we do meet the conditions, then we can and must expect all that God has promised. To do anything less is unbelief. That applies to the wicked just as it applies to the saved. God promises to those who are unsaved are just as real as the promises to those of us who are saved. Luke 13:3 says "Except you repent ye shall all likewise perish." That is a promise of God's word and it is real. John 3:18 reads, "He that believeth not is condemned already." To doubt the truth of that is to doubt he who said, I am truth. Do you believe that? Then, if we believe let us persuade men to believe on him. God's promises to the wicked shall be made true, just as real as God's promises to those who are saved.

What about God's promises to those who do believe. The scripture says in Revelation 21:7 "He that believeth shall inherit all things". If you believe then all things are yours. Not some but all. You have a right to believe and a right to accept that promise of God. That includes temporal things. David said in Psalms 37:25, "I have been young and now I am old and I have never seen the righteous or his seed begging bread". God said I'll give you the temporal things that you need. "Seek ye first the kingdom of God and all these things shall be added unto you", Matthew 6:33. That includes spiritual things as well. Do you doubt the assurance of your salvation? Do you doubt whether or not you are saved?

Assurance comes from God, and God says, thy sins are forgiven. The Lord reigneth, let the earth rejoice; let the multitude of isles be glad thereof. Psalms 97:1 and Revelation 19:6 say, "... Alleluia: for the Lord God omnipotent reigneth." Have faith in God.

The apostle Paul was on a ship one time and God had given him a special revelation. He was talking to the sailors and they asked, "What will we do?" Paul said these words, "... I believe God..." Paul anchored his soul on those three words, I believe God. Then he comes along and says for all of us, have faith in God, but base your faith upon the promises of the Word of God which liveth and abideth forever. Don't accept the testimony of man, but be reasonable, have a logical faith and make sure your faith is based upon the Word of God, and then expect all things which God has promised unto you. Do not expect those things that God has denied.

Have faith in God. That is the demand of logical faith. Faith turns God just like the needle of the compass turns to the polar star. Have faith in God. Reason may sit on the throne of an intellect, but faith wears the crown of the throne. Have faith in God.

Prayer: Our heavenly father, we praise you for thy word. We thank you for the instruction of thy word. Father, help us not to be carried about as the waves of the sea to and fro with every wind of doctrine. Help us to be men of faith. Help us to be encouraged enough to get hold of thee by our faith. Father help us also to base our faith on the word of God which liveth and abideth forever. Help us to understand thy word has said, except ye repent, ye shall all likewise perish. That's a promise of God. Help us father to have faith in that. Help us to accept the testimony of your word and then when the word says thy shall have all things, spiritual and temporal; help us to place our faith in those words. Lord help us not to try to undermine the word of God. Help us not to run through the scriptures and prostitute it. Help us father not to take from them that which they will not yield. We ask that you help us place our lives in the center of thy will so that when we pray we have faith to believe that the promises are ours. If there is one here that does not know Christ as their personal Savior, I pray that their faith might be strong enough to believe the testimony of the word of God. I pray for that one that is backslidden, that they might have faith to believe the promises of God's word which says, if we confess our sins, he is faithful and just to forgive us our sin and cleanse us from all unrighteousness. We demand no more. We expect no more than your word allows. Have your own way in our hearts and lives and we will praise you for it, in the name of Jesus and for it is in his name we pray. Amen.

11

The Great White Throne Judgment

Revelation 20:11

Revelation 20:11 is not a very pleasant scripture, in fact it is not a pleasant fact to look forward to. I wish it wasn't there. I truly wish today that there was not a hell to shun. I wish that we could live our lives under the Christian principle. I am not glad there is a hell. My soul shrinks from it, but yet, I know that it is there. Hell does exist. The word of God teaches it and I believe the word of God.

Therefore, I want you to hear it, not with your ears, but I want you to hear it with your understanding. I want you to hear it with your heart, your soul, hear it with your emotions - The scripture concerning the Great White Throne Judgment.

Revelation 20:11 "And I saw a great white throne, and him that sat on it, from whose face the earth and the heaven fled away; and there was found no place for them."

It is wonderful to think about the Lord Jesus Christ as being gentle; as being our shepherd. We love to think of him as being the one who loves us and died for us and guides us. But there is another part to the life of Jesus. That is, according to the word of God, Jesus is not only gentle, meek and mild, Jesus shall be a judge. The fact that God is a God of Judgment is a fact of history. God judged Adam when he sinned against that which he knew to be right. God judged the angels; God judged Lucifer and banished him from heaven because of his rebellion against the very throne of God. God judged the Roman Empire, God judged Hitler, God is a judge that is coming again with vengeance and judgment upon them that know not the Lord. I don't mean those who do not know him in sort of an easy believe way, but those who have not confessed, repented of their sin, and received Jesus into their heart and life as Savior and as Lord.

The scripture says he is coming again to judge and to bring vengeance upon those who have not had that experience. There are several distinct judgments listed in the scripture. There will be the judgment of the Jew, judgment of the nations, the judgment of the saved, the judgment of the dead and judgment of the unsaved to mention a few. Revelation 20:11 is describing a particular kind of judgment referred to as the Great White Throne Judgment. At this judgment, the saved will not be there. At this judgment only those that have rejected Christ as Savior will appear at the Great White Throne Judgment. As we think about the judgment, there are two or three things we need to notice.

First of all, who will be judged? God says that he has committed all judgment unto the Son. Think of it – this same Jesus of whom we sing 'Jesus loves me this I know for the Bible tells me so...' or Jesus gentle, meek and mild is the same Jesus that God has committed judgment to. He offers himself today as our lawyer, our advocate to stand in the midst of the throne and plead our case. But in that day, he shall be our judge.

There is an illustration that I read some time ago and it is supposed to be true. A young man was on a sled during the snowy weather. He was going down a hill, lost control of it and was headed straight for an automobile. A man standing to the side saw what was about to happen and he rushed into the situation to save this young boy from certain death. In the days to come, this young man went into a life of crime. Finally, he was arrested and brought before the judge. When he walked into the courthouse his eyes lit up when he saw that the judge was the man who saved his life. He said to himself, "I've got it made. This man saved my life once, he will do it again." The jury heard the case, they directed that this young man pay for his crime with his life and that he receive the death penalty. This young man was sure that the judge would not take that recommendation. The judge, after hearing the facts of the case, pronounced the death sentence upon that young man. The young man rose to his feet and said, "But your honor, you saved my life once." The judge responded, "Yes son in that day I was your savior, but today I must be your judge.

When Jesus came the first time, he stood before Pilate. He was judged by Pilate and when he comes again, Pilate will stand before Jesus and be judged. It seems to me that it does a lot of folks good or some kind of good for their egos to come to church and sit in the congregation as judge and jury and decide that Jesus Christ is not worthy to be their Savior. The Bible says that one day we shall stand before the judge and the judge in that day will be that one who gave his life as our Savior. In that day, he will become our judge. When you stand before Jesus Christ, the scripture says that what he does with us will be determined by what we did with him.

You can settle that. You can settle what Jesus Christ will do with you. The scripture says, "Whosoever shall confess me before men, him will I confess before my father which is in heaven. He who denies me before man, he will I deny before my Father which is in heaven. You can settle your destiny. You can settle the fact whether you will stand before The Great White Throne Judgment or not. The invitation is to receive the Lord Jesus Christ as your Savior rather than postpone him and let him be your judge.

The scripture says "every knee shall bow and every tongue will confess that He is Christ to the glory of the Father." Some people have said, 'preacher, the scripture says that one day I'll bow my knee before God and confess him as Lord. Therefore, I am going to have another opportunity. If I am going to bow my knee then I am going to be saved. 'You have to really work at misunderstanding scripture like that. You have to work at being stupid. You see, all of us were created for one reason. Every one of us was created for the purpose of bringing honor and glory to God's Son, the Lord Jesus Christ and you will honor Him. I will glorify him. I will either do that in one of two ways. I will recognize that I am lost and I am a sinner and deserve to go to hell and I cry out to Jesus for mercy and receive him as my Savior and therefore glorifying him and honoring him as Lord. Or, I can postpone that – I can push Jesus into the background and someday I will bow my knee and confess him as judge. One way or the other, I will honor him and glorify him. Either willingly as my Savior, or forced to it as my judge. You can decide that today.

Every knee shall bow. Jesus, the Son of man, the scripture says, has the power on Earth to forgive sin. That means now, that means today. Whosoever shall call upon the Lord shall be saved. He has the power to forgive sin. If we recognize him as Savior and we receive him then we have confessed him as Savior. It is a willing, loving confession as Savior and Lord of our lives. But in that day, when every knee shall bow, it will be a confession not to salvation but a confession that he is my judge. Jesus says today is the day and now is the time of salvation. You may look over him and you may ignore him, you may push him into the background, but one day your knee will bow and you can decide how you will bow that knee – as Savior or as judge. He will be the judge.

Secondly, who are going to be judged? John said, "And I saw the dead small and great stand before the throne." Revelation 20:12. Folks have a twisted idea about those folks that are lost. They fully expect to see the bums in hell; they fully expect to see the murders, the whoremonger, and the adulterer. They fully expect to see the skid row crowd in hell. John says, I saw the kings, I saw the high and mighty, the society crowd, the small and the great stand before the throne. All in one company both the small and great. The dead means the unsaved. They may have been physically alive, but dead spiritually when Jesus came. The scripture says that when the dead were there, both small and great, that the books were opened. In that day, there will be no place to hide. I wonder, I wish I could know or I think I wish I could know how many people go to church today to hide in the presence of others there. They use church to hide from God. Men come to church and they laugh, giggle and punch one another in the ribs and judge themselves by those who are not there. You see he didn't go to church and I did, type attitude. People like that take security in the fact that they are in the house of God someone else is not.

The scripture says that during the Great White Throne Judgment, you will be alone with no place to hide. The books were open. The books, I believe, were the books of opportunity as well, as books recording our works. I believe, that just as surely as I live that in that day God, in some way, will show across the screen of heaven every opportunity that the unsaved had to be saved. I believe that you will remember every radio preacher you heard, every prayer you heard, every visitor that came and knocked on your door, every time you heard the preacher preach, you will remember that when you stand before God in the Great White Throne Judgment.

Revelation 20:15 'And whosoever was not found written in the book of life was cast into the lake of fire." Christians will not be there. Those who have been born again will not stand in the Great White Throne. They will stand later at the Judgment Seat of Christ to receive the rewards done for their service for God. The White Throne is reserved for those who reject the Lord.

Finally, the judgment itself, as in any trial, there is going to be witnesses. Many will come and witness against those who rejected the Lord Jesus Christ. It will not be a question of works. Works will not count in this judgment. The books of opportunity of your salvation will be opened. There is a book in which the blood of the Lord Jesus Christ has written those who have been born again. In this book will be an ugly blank of those whose name might have been written but rejected the Lord. I believe that God will show you the blood of Christ and the pen of his love dipped in that blood that would have recorded your name in the Lamb's Book of Life. But you did not receive that love. The witnesses will come. I believe that some preachers will be called to be witnesses and they are going to say Lord I preached the best way I knew how and I urged them, not from a standpoint of hatred or rejoicing that there was a hell, but I, with a heart of love, pleaded for them to be saved. I urged them to receive Christ as their personal Savior, but they would not. The Holy Spirit will be called as a witness and he is going to say I tugged at their hearts day and night, I showed them over and over again. I pulled at the strings of their heart when they heard that gospel song or when they heard that sermon. I was there Lord and I was faithful to tug at their heart, but they would not. I believe that Sunday school teachers and God help a Sunday school teacher who doesn't teach the gospel of the Lord Jesus Christ. God help a Sunday school teacher who doesn't love and long for the salvation of their students. I believe there will be Sunday school teachers that will say I loved him as a child and I pleaded with him or her to receive Christ as their Savior but they wouldn't. I believe the Lord himself will open his hands and the scars on his hands and feet and his side will be a witness against those who said no to Jesus.

Some will say, I didn't have the opportunity to be saved. And God is going to say just a minute, just a minute, let me show you on the screen of heaven the times, the opportunities you had to bow that knee and receive me as Savior. Somebody else is going to say, but Lord I was a good man. I lived a good life, Lord. Jesus will say yes, but I never told you that you got saved by doing good, but you were saved by faith receiving me as your Savior. Remember the time when you heard that sermon about your righteousness being as filthy rags. Do you remember the time you heard the sermon that the heart of man is deceitful above all things and desperately wicked? You remember when the preacher said all have sinned and come short of the glory of God; and when he said the wages of sin is death, but the gift of God is eternal life through Jesus Christ our Lord. Remember those times? But Lord, I gave to the Red Cross, the United Way, the Kidney Foundation and everything that came through town and I supported them. Whosoever's name was not written in the Lamb's Book of Life was cast into the lake of fire. But Lord, I intended to do it, tomorrow I was going to be saved. Whosoever's name was not written in the Lamb's Book of Life was cast into the lake of fire. The verdict of the Great White Throne Judgment will be Guilty, Guilty, and Guilty!

And over and over again, it will cry out from your mind every silver studded nail in every door of the penitentiary of hell will echo, Guilty! Guilty! Guilty! The angels will bow their heads and turn their backs as they see the damned bound and cast into the lake of fire. They too shall say guilty, guilty, and guilty! The Bible doesn't say that you will be condemned at the Great White Throne Judgment; the Bible says you are condemned already, because you have not believed on the Son of God.

I hold him up before you today. There is no need for anyone to ever stand before the judgment that I have described. It is for those who reject Jesus, reserved for that particular individual; not for those who know him. And I wish it wasn't there. I wish there was no such thing as hell. I wish there was no such thing as the Great White Throne Judgment, but wishes don't change the word of God – it is there. You can escape and you can rejoice in the fact that you will live forever with Jesus, by receiving him as your personal Savior.

On this side of judgment, you are saved just as you are. By bowing a knee and saying Lord, I'm guilty, I confess and just as I am I come to thee. On the other side, the judgment will be just as you are without God, without Christ, without hope. And instead of being Savior to save you just as you are, he will be judge to judge you just as you are. Come to the Lord, Come to Jesus just as you are. He will save you; he died for you and he wants you to be saved. He waits to save you today.

Prayer: Heavenly Father, we thank you for the word of God. We realize there is much in the word of God that is not pleasant. It is not pleasant for those who have rejected Jesus Christ; it is not pleasant for those who are Christians. It is a fact that no amount of reasoning can cover up. No amount of translations can take it from the Word of God for it is there. Father, I pray today that we might have the good sense to believe what our hearts have felt and what our eyes have read. Help us Father to make a sound, reasonable decision to receive Christ as our personal Savior. If there is one who does not know the Lord, I pray that today will be the time that they will bow that knee lovingly before you and receive your Son as their Savior. Father, you move and help us for there is nothing more we can do. On this side of judgment, you are saved just as you are. By bowing a knee and saying Lord, I am guilty I confess and just as I am I come to thee. On the other side of judgment will be just as you are without God, without Christ and without hope. Instead of being Savior to save you just as you are, he will judge and judge you just as you are. Come to the Lord, Come to Jesus, just as you are. He will save you. He died for you. He wants you to be saved. He waits to save you now. Take this invitation, and move your people and those who do not know you and I'll praise you and thank you for what you are going to do in Jesus name. Amen

12

The Divine Flow of Love

I John 4: 7-19

I want to talk about something very personal to me and that God has worked into my spirit in the years of my pastorate. Beloved, God will confirm his word. If you find a scripture, no matter how difficult it is to translate, understand or whether it is very simple, if you meditate on that verse and have a will to know what God's will is, God will confirm in your own personal experience that verse of scripture. You will be able to say God can confirm His word, that scripture is real in my life. I want to share something that is so simple, I almost hesitate to preach it. It is so void of any kind of weights, it is just as simple as it can be, but God has worked it into my life in a very special way. I believe it will be a help to you as Christians and your relationship to one another.

I John 4: 7 - 19 says, "Beloved, let us love one another: for love is of God; and every one that loveth is born of God, and knoweth God. He that loveth not knoweth not God; for God is love. In this was manifested the love of God toward us, because that God sent his only begotten Son into the world, that we might live through him. Herein is love, not that we loved God, but that he loved us, and sent his Son to be the propitiation for our sins. Beloved, if God so loved us, we ought also to love one another. No man hath seen God at any time. If we love one another, God dwelleth in us, and his love is perfected in us. Hereby know we that we dwell in him, and he in us, because he hath given us of his Spirit. And we have seen and do testify that the Father sent the Son to be the Savior of the world. Whosoever shall confess that Jesus is the Son of God, God dwelleth in him, and he in God. And we have known and believed the love that God hath to us. God is love; and he that dwelleth in love dwelleth in God, and God in him. Herein is our love made perfect, that we may have boldness in the Day of Judgment: because as he is, so are we in this world. There is no fear in love; but perfect love casteth out fear: because fear hath torment. He that feareth is not made perfect in love. We love him, because he first loved us."

As I said, I want to share something that is tremendously personal. There are some things that I want to rehearse with you in our text. First of all, perfect love casts out fear. There is a translation that says, Perfect love turns fear out of doors. It is sort of like it has, in the picture in my mind, that when you go to bed at night you go to the door, take the cat, open the door, pitch him outside and shut the door. One translation says perfect love takes fear to the door and kicks it out.

Secondly, we need to grow in love. We are admonished to grow in love. To begin our relationships with one another may be very trying at times, but if we become Christians and dwell together for a long period of time, our love for one another has to grow and mature. Because God is love and nobody has seen God at any time and if we experience and express love, God dwells in that and we dwell in him.

Thirdly, we need to walk in love. We need to follow after love and we must be guided by love. God is a big God. You cannot take God and put him in a box and say, here is God; or put him in a corner and say this is God. God is God and he can do anything he wants to do, can't he? There are ways we express who God is and talk about his many attributes. He is omniscient, all knowing. He is omnipotent, he has all power and he is immutable, he is holy, but the greatest is God is love.

In the 1960's and early 70's the hippies came through town. There was something about them that many of us recall. We didn't like their lifestyle; we didn't agree with their lifestyle. But, I'll tell you brother, when they stopped you on the street corner and handed you a track and said to you, ' God is Love', they told you a very beautiful thing. That was their method, God loves you. And when they said that they were expressing a very precious thing for the scripture says, God is love.

I want to share with you something God showed me in the passage of scripture that I call the divine flow of love. I want to try to share with you and try to get you to understand what I mean by the divine flow of love. There are two kingdoms in the world, brethren. There is the kingdom of darkness. From that kingdom comes a stream of hatred, sorrow, sickness, confusion, conceit, envy, jealousy and all those other things. The ruler of that kingdom is Satan. The other kingdom is the kingdom of Light. From that kingdom comes a stream of love, peace, joy and understanding. The ruler of that kingdom is God.

There is a stream of love flowing from the kingdom of light to your heart. That stream, like a great search light from the sky, comes into your heart, goes out of you and lights your path. The scripture says walk in love. Follow after love. Be guided by love. And there flows today from that kingdom of light a stream of divine love and compassion into your heart as a child of God. We are going to talk about what you do with it when it comes into your heart. Perfect love casts out fear. The devil wants you to believe that everything you tremble at and everything you have fear over is of God. He wants you to think that which causes you to tremble comes from the kingdom of light. That is just not so. It comes from Satan. There are times when we can't distinguish between the voice of God and the voice of Satan. I admit that there are times when there are problems in areas trying to understand for sure if it is God leading me to do this or is it Satan trying to deceive me.

It is generally true, I think, that a good judge of what to do is found in that verse, 'Perfect love casts out fear'. When that which is perfect, the love of God, comes into your heart, there is no fear about the decision you have to make. God takes away the fear and worry and he gives you peace about a matter you have to make a decision over.

Generally speaking, wherever the devil is there is fear. Wherever God is there is love. When my wife says to me, I love you it does not make me tremble. It makes my heart beat a little fast, but not tremble in fear. When she says to me, ' I love you', I don't run off and hide somewhere. It is a joy and comfort to me for my wife to express her love to me. When I tell my children I love them, they don't run off and hide. They don't go to bed and have nightmares. But where Satan is there is fear.

Now I want you to understand I am not talking about a ha ha kind of love. I am not talking about a frivolous love. Love is not to be understood as a car going down the highway painted with daisies and the words, make love not war painted on it. That was used as a symbol of love in years past. That is not what I am talking about. I am talking about the perfect love of God. How many of you can honestly say, Brother Boyd I know my heart and I want to be used of God. I don't know where, I don't know how but if I know my heart, I want to be used of God. I don't know where and I don't know how to find out where or how. That is a problem for many Christians. If you want to be used of God and you don't know how, I want to tell you something very precious that will allow you to do the will of God and know for sure. The scripture says when a man feels love he feels God. A man who walks after love, is following love and is guided by love, will be led of God. There was a time in my life and it began when I was very small. There would come time I could not explain it. I had to look back on it to explain it. There were times in my life when I was small, times when there would well up in me some of the most tender precious intimate thoughts about somebody. There seemed to be something all of the sudden, without any apparent reason, that someone would come to my mind. I would begin to think about that person and I would, it seemed, to swell up with compassion of love. I could not understand or explain.

The first time I experienced that was when I was a freshman in high school. It was then that I began to really know what it was. But I had experienced it many times before. One time during a Christmas party in the high school cafeteria presents were handed out and I was lucky if I received one. On Valentine's Day, all the boys would get a box full of valentines and I would get one. The teacher would give me one. At Christmas, if whoever got my name happened to be there that day, I would get a present because otherwise I would not. We had about 54 people in our class and had punch and cookies and exchanged gifts. They brought me my gift that had been wrapped in aluminum foil. I opened it and found a box of chocolate covered cherries. Now being an old farm boy and not going to town very often, I could have eaten every one of them right there. We had a fellow in our class who was very quiet and his first name was Raymond. Raymond was very shy and an excellent student. He made straight A's but stayed to himself. The rest of us were laughing and carrying on and I looked and he did not have a gift. Nobody brought him anything. Kids can be so cruel to each other and they can hurt one another by being thoughtless. Kids use to walk up behind me at the water fountain at school and say, 'what size shoe do you really wear?' I notice Raymond walk through the crowd very slowly with his head bowed and he went outside. He began to walk out through the school yard and I thought my heart would burst. There went out to him such a love and compassion that nearly broke my heart. I got one of the teachers and ask them if they had any wrapping paper. I asked her to wrap my box of chocolate covered cherries and put his name on it. She did and I went running out to him, yelling comeback here. I told him the biggest lie I had ever told. I told him that when we brought the gifts up we left his under the tree down in Mrs. Nannie Harris's room. He smiled from ear to ear. And when I walked away that day I know I heard God say to me, "You are a good kid". I want to be a son that brings pleasure to my father's heart, don't you? That is what Jesus wanted to do. "I do always those things which please my father". He was a father pleaser. Sometimes we ought to take our prayer lists and tear them up and just kneel and say Father today let me be a son or daughter that brings pleasure to your heart.

Do you know why I felt so good that day? Not because I had done something that was not selfish, but that I had experienced God. God is love, is that not what the scripture says? He who feels love, feels God. And as that young skinny freshman, I experienced the creator of the universe. I felt him move in my heart. The scripture says grow in love. Follow after love and be guided by love. It is a marvelous thing to experience God. That stream of love came down from heaven and into my heart and flowed out to that one who was being hurt by a friend.

You may say, Preacher, I want to be guided by God, then be guided by love. I want to be guided by the Holy Spirit, then be guided by love. God is love. Have you ever had the question in your mind what does God want me to do? Who does God want me to minister to today? Who does God want me to speak to? What do I say to somebody? Where does God want me to go and to whom do I need to minister today? And you have experienced from time to time, the love of God spread abroad in your heart by the Holy Spirit. There was that dwelling up inside. You may have to look back to see it, but you have experienced it. You know what I am talking about.

The scripture says never follow hate. Don't ever follow that spirit of getting even. That is the devil. It is not of God. Never return evil for evil because that belongs to Satan. Follow that stream and be guided by it. It is God. We make it so complicated. We make this thing of knowing God and living in Christ so complicated at times that we take all the joy out of it. It is so simple and so sweet and precious. God will confirm it if we just walk in it.

How many of you while at work suddenly, without any apparent reason, feel and think about someone. You begin to have tender thoughts about someone. How many of you ever felt that? You said, I wonder how Mrs. Sarah is doing today. I haven't talked to her in two weeks, wonder how she is doing? All of the sudden, for no reason at all, you see somebody in your mind and say to yourself I wonder how that person is doing. Have you had someone come up to you and tell you they were thinking about you yesterday? I have people say that to me and could, under my breath, say Brother, I could have used you yesterday to when you were thinking about me. Listen, if that feeling ever comes again, I don't care what you are doing, you quit doing it and bake a pie; get into your car go see them and hug their neck. You do something, you go because you are experiencing God. God wants you to minister to someone and that is the only way he can get you there.

Many of you have felt it and missed it and let it slip. All of those experiences are from God. It flows from heaven into your heart and goes out to whom you are thinking about. God would have used you many times, if you had been obedient to that which you were feeling in your heart, but you let it slip. I said that this is very intimate and very personal and I will explain. One day, I was in my car driving out Opryland Drive about in front of the Opryland Hotel coming from lunch and on my way to make another call. As I was driving along, for no particular reason, my brother who was three years older than me, seemed to be sitting in the car with me. I hadn't seen him in months. Our family is not that close. I thought to myself how he is doing and I wonder why I thought of him. I continued to drive and it was about noon. I continued to have him on my mind the rest of the afternoon. I began to think about the times we were little and time we would fight like cats and dogs. I remembered the good times and suddenly there were tears in my eyes because I was thinking about him in the most intimate and personal way. At 2 p.m. that afternoon they rushed him to the hospital and they were fighting to save his life. He had gotten a prescription of the strongest valium you can buy. He took the whole prescription. The very moment I had those feelings, he was in trouble. He was in a crisis and God would have moved me but I didn't listen. I shrugged it off. When I was driving to the hospital the only thing I could say was, 'God forgive me, I missed it'. I missed it. When I got there they were beating on his chest with their fists and shocking him and tried to bring him back to life. I thought he wasn't going to make it. I was feeling God. God is love. He who feels love, feels God. How many of you have ever missed it? Be honest, you felt it but you went right on with what you were doing. It will make a difference in your life.

Preacher, how do I get that kind of love? How do I get in that kind of condition that I might know God's love? If you heart is filled with covetousness; if you are mean in your spirit; if you have tension in your home, you will never feel what I'm talking about. The scripture says that we cannot know bitterness and have bitterness in our heart and know God at the same time. Bitterness and sweetness does not come from the same fountain. You have heard the expression don't let the sun go down on your wrath. Don't harbor anger in your heart. How many of you fellows had to beat the sun home? Some of us had to do that. You can't handle ill feelings and anger, tension and feel what I am talking about.

If you keep your heart clean and you keep your heart filled with love, you will experience love. If there is bitterness in your heart get it removed. If there is resentment in your heart confess it for the sin that it is. Let Jesus heal you. Make peace and the love of God will flow into your heart. You want to love God today? You want to follow love? God is love. If you follow where love is flowing to the end of the stream you will find Christ there. I guarantee it. If you will just follow it, there he will be at the end.

Where should I go? What should I do? Just get love in your heart, don't manufacture it. We Christians have a willpower screw, you know, somewhere and we screw that down real tight when we've got to do this or that. Just get love in your heart. Love God and love people and when it comes follow it. God will send you to the very person he wants you to minister to.

You know why we don't win souls? We don't win souls because we don't go where God wants us to go. God has to prepare that person. You can be at your office at noon today and all of the sudden you have a feeling in your heart toward someone who is unsaved. If you will go right then, you will win that person to the Lord. But if you wait till Thursday night at 7 p.m., and you go out and knock on doors and pray no one is there, you are not going to win anybody to the Lord. If you get your heart full of love, God will send you to the one he wants you to go to and you won't have to say much when you get there.

A few years ago, there was a woman in our church and she had six children. The husband of that family was a big tall fellow, he was a good 6'6" and weighed about 250, all man. He was a rough rascal. He lived just as far up on Cemetery Ridge back out on the bluff as you could get off of Marrowbone Road. His wife and those children would come to church every Sunday. She would come in and a whole line of kids would follow. On a Monday, I began to feel this compassion, I have been talking about, toward this man. I wanted him to be saved more than anyone in this world. To be honest, I was afraid to go see him. I was afraid he would hit me. I was in camp and told another man about this feeling toward this man. He said let's pray and let's thank God that this love you have in your heart is going to lead you to this man. And next Sunday, this man is going to find Christ as his personal Savior. At first I thought this was putting God out on a limb. I came home Wednesday night and announced we were going to see a miracle Sunday. Praise God there is going to be a miracle right here in church. I really thought there would be. I prayed all week, thanking God for this man being saved on Sunday. All that week the love kept going out to him. Sunday, when I got up to preach, the back door opened and here came the wife and all six children and he wasn't with them. My heart sank. I just knew he was going to be there, walk the aisle, and shout and all these things and he wasn't even there. I thought to myself I still had tonight. Sunday night came, back door opened and the mother and her children entered without him. I told the church I could not deliver on what I had advertised. We are not going to see the miracle. I must have prayed wrong or I prayed selfish or something went wrong and I apologized. Somebody said, brother the day is not over yet. I got in my car and drove up that dark road and the only thing I could feel was the love in my heart for that man. I had to get to him; I had to see him; I just had to go. I drove down Marrowbone Road turned off onto a gravel road and went straight up to the top of the hill. I was rehearsing to myself what I would say to him. I got to his house and got out of my car and went in. I sat down in the living room and he was in the kitchen. His wife told him I was there to see him. He came in and God whispered in my ear, don't blow this one. I said to him, Brother, I don't know why I am here tonight except to tell you that I love you with all my heart. He was sitting in his recliner and just folded up right out in the floor and said, "I have been waiting for a long time for someone to tell me that". He prayed and received Christ into his heart. He went to the phone and called his son and said, "I just got saved". His son was a Free Will Baptist preacher. Brother, God will confirm his word. If I had gone to visit the man on the designated Thursday visitation night, I would have not been able to reason with than man. We make it so complicated. It is so simple. God is love and he who feels love feels God.

Did you ever pass by a man sitting on a street corner with a cup in his lap and something goes out toward that person? You are experiencing God. God is saying to you minister to that man. Don't wait till lightning strikes you. God is love and he wants you to minister. If you follow after it, it is so simple. You can go to church, shout, praise God and talk about God and you can exalt yourself and your program, but you will never feel God. 1 Corinthians 13 says after listing all the great things he says the greatest of these is love. You can learn it all, you can have it all, but if your heart is not filled with love you are nothing. You are a zero with the rim rubbed off. Did you ever feel like a zero with the rim rubbed off?

There was a young man in school one time and he had a Christian professor. The professor was trying to get this fellow to get a revelation of God. The student said, "I don't believe God exists". He told the student to go out in the backyard and look up into the sky and say these words, "God, if there is a God, reveal yourself to me." The boy said if I catch everyone out of sight, I might do it. That night the boy goes out and does what the professor asked him to do. The next day in class, the professor asked the student if he did what he was asked to do. The boy said, I went out and said, "God, if there is a God, I want to know you." He told the professor he felt like a fool. The professor said that's a good revelation for a beginner.

Stay full of love. When your family turns you out, stay full of love. When they hurt you stay full of love. Don't follow mysteries and don't follow fleeces, brother. Listen fleeces have got me in more trouble than I could get out of in 40 years. You are close to tempting God when you put out a fleece. Follow love and Jesus will be where the flow is.

Do you have a genuine love in your heart today? Do you have a Godly love? I want to ask you today, if you don't have that genuine, Godly love to ask God to remove everything in your heart except genuine love. Take away the bitterness, the resentment, take it out of your heart and ask God to fill you with love. If you want to see souls saved, get full of love. This love flows all away around the world. There have been missionaries on a foreign field that were in a crisis and someone back in the states woke up at midnight and all of the sudden they think about these people. They get down beside their bed and pray and at that very moment that missionary was needing prayer.

A man, in Nashville, called a friend who worked in the Free Will Baptist denomination and said I was thinking about you today and wondered how you were doing. The friend told him the next day that when he called he was writing his letter of resignation. I was going to hang it up and quit. This fellow just called for no apparent reason and told his friend he appreciated the good job he was doing. When you feel that love, there is someone somewhere in a particular crisis and God is the only one who knows anything about it. God is trying to move you to minister to that person.

Get full of love today. God is reaching out to you right now. God so loved the world that he gave his only begotten Son that whosoever believeth in him shall not perish but have everlasting life. For herein is love not that we love God but that God loved us. God commendeth his love toward us that while we were yet sinners, Christ died for us. Follow love and where the flow stops you will find Jesus.

Prayer: Heavenly father we thank you for confirming your word. We thank you that you have in our own experience made real and beyond a shadow of doubt what your word declares. Father, help us to not be so complicated about this thing of serving you. No man hath seen God at any time, but he that dwells in God, God dwells in him and is manifest. God help us to get our hearts full of love and follow it that you might lead us to that person whose heart is broken; to that soul that is lost; to that one who is in need. We don't have to know all the ins and outs of how to deal with people and all the physiology just go with love and say what I said. God I want to love this person and help me to love them through me and you love them through me. And just say those sweet words, I love you and God loves you. Then watch the Holy Spirit work in their lives. For Father it is so simple and we thank you for it. Now there may be those who in their heart need to cleanse their heart of everything except genuine love and there may be someone without Christ and that love is flowing to them right now, help them to walk the aisle guided by that stream of love and help them to find Jesus at the end. We ask that you minister to us now as we wait before you in these precious moments. We pray in the name of Jesus. Amen.

13

The Blood of Christ

I John 1:7

"But if we walk in the light, as he is in the light, we have fellowship one with another, and the blood of Jesus Christ, his Son, cleanseth us from all sin." Snowfall reminds me of the pure white holiness, righteousness of Christ in shedding His blood that our sins may be washed away. I began to think about the blood of Jesus Christ and want to share this message with you.

I John 1:7 says the blood of Jesus Christ, his Son, cleanses us from all sin. I was talking to a young minister not too awful long ago and we were talking about a particular doctrine, a particular subject of the Bible and he said to me, "I don't preach on that and the reason I don't preach on that is because I myself do not understand it. I have studied it, I have read the scriptures, I have read cross references, commentaries and I am still not convinced in my own heart that I understand it." I suppose that it is not good to talk about something that you don't know anything about or that you don't feel comfortable with, but did you ever stop to think that if the preacher just preached on parts of the Bible that he understood there wouldn't be much preaching. There are a lot of things in the scripture I do not understand, there are some things I take by faith, though I cannot explain them. That is, I cannot tell you what God had in his mind or heart in many different incidences. Some things are beyond my comprehension. But I have found that God will bless a fellow if he will just preach what the scripture says whether he understands it or not. One such scripture is found dealing with the sacrifice of God's Son. I don't understand how God loved us enough to do that. I do not understand how God came to that conclusion. I don't understand how one man could die for the sin of all, but I believe that he did – I believe that Jesus Christ died for my sin and I believe that if I believe on Him as my personal Savior that my faith is counted unto me as righteousness. Though I may not fully understand it or able to explain it to you, my job is to proclaim what the word of God says. In I John 1:7 when it says, the blood of his Son cleanses us from all sin, I know, though I cannot explain it perfectly, that he is talking about the actual blood of the Lord Jesus Christ. He is not spiritualizing. He is not using some kind of metaphor. He is not using some figure of speech, but he is talking about the actual blood of the Lord Jesus Christ. The least effective preaching in the world is what we call spiritualizing. Spiritualizing is taking a passage of scripture and spiritualize it to mean something else and to let folks use their imagination. But the word of God says what it says and we must declare it. And that portion of scripture which speaks of the blood of the Lord Jesus Christ means the actual blood of Jesus Christ.

I do not understand why many of the denominational churches today are taking out of their hymn books those hymns that deal with the blood. You cannot spiritualize and take away what they laughingly call slaughter house religion. It is the actual blood of Jesus. John answered that philosophy which said Jesus Christ was just a man. John declared that in the beginning was the word and that word became flesh and it dwelt among us. Then there were those who, when they saw that they could not destroy the faith of man, came back with another kind of philosophy in John's day. They said he was divine, that he was indeed an angelic form. He was not man, but an angel. John wrote in I John 5:6- 9 these words, "This is he that came by water and by blood even Jesus Christ; not by water only but by water and blood and it is the spirit that beareth witness because the spirit is truth. For there are three that bear record in heaven, the Father, the Word, and the Holy Ghost: and these three are one. And there are three that bear witness in earth, the Spirit, and the water, and the blood: and these three agree in one. If we receive the witness of men, the witness of God is greater: for this is the witness of God which he hath testified of his Son." John answered those who would challenge men's faith. So when the Bible talks about the blood of Jesus Christ, it is talking about the actual blood of Jesus Christ. It is the tangible, crimson red blood; blood that you could touch. It was the blood that you could find in a pool at the foot of the cross. It was the blood you could have filled a basin with at the foot of the cross. You could have wiped the blood from his brow. He is actually talking about the actual blood that flowed through the veins of the one who was the God man. He was God if he was not man and he was truly man as if he was not God. John 19:34 - 35 reads, "But one of the soldiers with a spear pierced his side, and forthwith came there out blood and water. And he that saw it bare record, and his record is true: and he knoweth that he saith true, that ye might believe". He said I saw the soldier as he took that spear and plunged it into the side of Jesus and I saw coming out of that wound blood and water and I bare record, he said, and my record is true. If we could ask Mary, mother of Jesus, she could tell you that it was really blood. As she stood at the cross, Jesus looked down and said to John, "John take my mother. Take Mary and let her be your mother, take her to your house. What agony and suffering that mother had to endure as she watched her Son being crucified on the cross.

Ask the soldiers; ask the centurion if it was real blood. They nailed his hands to the cross. They nailed his feet to the cross. Ask the witnesses in heaven. I John 5: 7-8 says "For there are three that bear record in heaven, the Father, The Word, and the Holy Ghost: and these three are one. And there are three that bear witness in earth, the Spirit, and the water, and the blood: and these three agree in one. So it was the actual blood of Jesus Christ. Not only was it the actual blood of the Lord Jesus Christ, but it was actually applied to your sin and to mine. Just as the priest of the Old

Testament days would take the blood of goats and wolves and so forth and sprinkle upon the people and upon that scapegoat. Once a year they carried it into the Holy of Holies and there apply it to the mercy seat, so was the blood of Jesus Christ actually applied to your sin and to mine. The writer of Hebrews says it perhaps more powerful than anyone else could have said it in Hebrews 9:11-14. "But Christ being come an high priest of good things to come, by a greater and more perfect tabernacle, not made with hands, that is to say, not of this building; Neither by the blood of goats and calves, but by his own blood he entered in once into the holy place, having obtained eternal redemption for us. For if the blood of bulls and of goats, and the ashes of a heifer sprinkling the unclean, sanctifieth to the purifying of the flesh: How much more shall the blood of Christ, who through the eternal Spirit offered himself without spot to God, purge your conscience from dead works to serve the living God?" The writer is saying just as there was an earthly sanctuary there is a heavenly sanctuary and just as the priest went once a year into this earthly tabernacle, so our high priest, Jesus Christ, went into that sanctuary in heaven. He went before God the Father in the courts of heaven and there he took his blood and actually applied it upon our sin. God looked at that sacrifice and accepted it as atonement or payment just as he accepted the sacrifice of the earthly priest. Christ shed his blood and put it on the altar before God in the sanctuary of heaven.

In the religion of the Jews today, they have many feasts. They have the Feast of Tabernacles, Feast of Dedication, and The Feast of the Passover and one day that is called the Fast Day. The Fast Day is the Day of Atonement. Once a year they celebrate this Day of Atonement. There was a day set aside in the history of Israel when the human priest would go once again into the Holy of Holies and apply the blood. The fact that the human priest had to go back every year signified his inability. They would take two goats, cast lots upon which one would die for the sin of the people. They would take that blood of that goat and sprinkle it upon the people and upon the altar and then they would take some remaining blood and put it on the other goat's head which was called a scapegoat. They would turn that goat loose to wander and be lost in the wilderness. All of it signifying that without the shedding of blood there is no redemption. At the same time signifying that no earthly priest and no blood of goats and calves could suffice. There had to come a time when there would be that perfect sacrifice, but it would have to be actual blood. It could not signify something; it had to be actual blood. It also had to be applied to our souls. The actual blood of the Lord Jesus Christ was actually applied and it brought forth an actual salvation. It brought forth a salvation you can know and feel. Brother, I praise God that there is such a thing as "know so" salvation. I use to think it sounded awfully spiritual and humble to go around saying, "I don't know if I am saved or not. I hope I am, I hope that when I get to heaven, I will be accepted." I use to think that was being humble. I used to laugh at Free Will Baptist, or any other, preacher who would say, "I am saved and I know I'm saved." I used to laugh at that kind of philosophy. But, brother, when you have had the blood of the Lord Jesus Christ applied to your heart, you know it, you feel it, and you can rejoice in it. Amen – you know you have been saved, you know that the blood of the Lamb has been applied to your heart; you know that there was an actual substitute who took your place and he paid the penalty. He died for us, he died in our stead. He died when you and I should have died. He took our place and received the judgment we should have received. He did it for us.

When Jesus was in prison there was a man by the name of Barabbas. He was a murderer and waiting his day of execution. He deserved to die and it was at that time when the Roman governor was obligated to turn lose someone to die to satisfy the pagan minds of those around. Barabbas knew this was his time, this was the time he would die while the people celebrated. Barabbas was in his cell and the Roman soldiers came, unlocked the door and said he was free to go. Barabbas must have thought, in his mind, there had been some terrible mistake, but he was free. Barabbas must have watched as they took Jesus and they marched him up the lonely road to Calvary. Surely, Barabbas saw Jesus Christ bearing the cross that he should have bore. He must have saw this man raised up on that center cross between two thieves and said to himself, "that's my cross; that is the one they had reserved for me, but there is someone dying on that cross in my place. Barabbas saw firsthand and understood atonement. Someone, though he did not receive it spiritually, saw it being played out before his very eyes. You and I deserve to die and carry that cross. You and I deserve to have our hands and feet nailed and our side pierced. You and I deserve the penalty, the judgment and the wrath of God, but Jesus took our place. As I stand before the cross, as Barabbas must have, as I look at those three crosses outlined against the sky, I can literally say the man on the center cross is on my cross. He took my place and is dying in my stead. Yes, it was the crimson blood of Jesus Christ that was actually applied and it brought an actual salvation.

Let me share with you a few verses of scripture: Romans 3:25 "Whom God hath set forth to be a propitiation through faith in his blood, to declare his righteousness for the remission of sins that are past, through the forbearance of God;" Romans 5:8 "But God commendeth his love toward us, in that, while we were yet sinners, Christ died for us. I Corinthians 15:3 says "For I delivered unto you first of all that which I also received, how that Christ died for our sins according to the scriptures;" I Corinthians 5:19 "If in this life only we have hope in Christ, we are of all men most miserable." Galatians 3:13 "Christ hath redeemed us from the curse of the law, being made a curse for us: for it is written, CURSED IS EVERY ONE THAT HANGETH ON A TREE." On and on we could go. Jesus Christ took our place. The beautiful thing about all of this is that salvation is available to the whole world. The Lord Jesus Christ shed his blood, the Lord God received the Son's blood and gave us an actual pardon. He gave us a deliverance from sin and freedom for all of us. The Word of God repeats that over and over again. Paul said that when we were yet sinners Christ died for us. In Ephesians 2:12 and 13 Paul said "That at the time ye were without Christ, being aliens from the commonwealth of Israel, and strangers from the covenants of promise, having no hope and without God in the world: but now in Christ Jesus ye who sometimes were far off are made nigh by the blood of Christ."

God accepted the blood of the Lord Jesus Christ as atonement for sin. Whatever man may be, whatever man may have done, praise God, he looks at the blood of the Lamb. The blood of the Lamb suffices, satisfied the justice of God. God always said and always will say, when I see the blood I will pass over you. Remember in Egypt during the Passover, God said to all those in Israel, whether Jew or not, that if they believed to take the blood from a lamb without spot or blemish, sacrifice that lamb and paint the blood over the door post of their house for the death angel will go throughout Egypt. God said when I see the blood, I will pass over you. He would visit every other house and the first born of every family would die, but when he saw the blood he would pass over.

Just suppose there was a man in Israel who believed God and did what God said. He went out and slew the best lamb he could find, took the blood and painted his doorpost and then sat in his house on that dreadful night and said, Oh God, I wonder if I've done enough. Lord, I wonder if my repentance were repentant enough. I wonder if my faith were faith enough. What a miserable night that man must have spent. Yet people today do the same thing. They hope they are saved. Brother, what a wretched miserable life to live a life not knowing and wondering if you did this right or that right. Your righteousness, your good life has nothing to do with salvation. Though it is reasonable to expect a man to live a good life, it has nothing to do with salvation. In reality, repentance and confession play a part in salvation. Nothing that comes from within us has to do with our salvation. God said when I see the blood, I will pass over you.

I could never be good enough. I could never have the kind of faith that I ought to have and that I owe God. So I must pray and pray earnestly, God if I'm ever saved, it must be by your grace and by your mercy. "For by grace are you saved through faith; and that not of yourselves: it is the gift of God: not of works, lest any man should boast," Ephesians 2:8-9. So I rest in the promises of God. As it says in the scriptures concerning the Israelites, he staggered not at the promises of God. Abraham heard all that God was going to do and he never once staggered at all those promises. I have to say as the book of Revelation says, unto him that loved us and washed us from our sin in his own blood to him be glory and dominion forever and forever. What a Savior – what a plan of salvation. The eternal promise that whosoever calleth on the name of the Lord believing in his heart and confessing his sin, repenting of his sin, believing in what God has done for him through Jesus Christ can come to the foot of the cross and there say to God, I believe. I apply the blood to my life and my soul, I see it. God would say in heaven, when I see the blood, I'll pass over.

Have you had the blood applied to your heart and life? Have you had the blood applied to your sin? Your sin can be washed as pure and as white as the snow in winter. Though your sins be as scarlet they shall be white as snow and though they be red like crimson they shall be as wool. Do you know him? Is he yours? If you have not had your heart applied with the blood, I invite you to come and actually partake of the actual shed blood of the Lord Jesus Christ.

Prayer: Father, we thank you this morning for the blood of Jesus Christ. We thank you that it was perfect and without spot or blemish. We praise you Father that it was of such quality that it satisfied a holy and just God. And Father we thank you we can feel and know in our hearts Jesus Christ walked into the Holy of Holies and into the sanctuary of heaven and there applied his blood to my sin. I praise you for a "know so" salvation. I thank you for the freedom and assurance that comes by knowing that the blood has been applied to my heart and life. If there is one here who does not know you or your Son, I pray today that they might come to this altar, that they might kneel and say, "Lord Jesus, I believe. Lord Jesus save me from sin". And then go away rejoicing having the blood applied. Father, meet the needs of every heart as you promised to do and we praise you now and throughout all eternity for what you accomplish through us. In the name of Jesus. Amen.

14

Coming Home

Jeremiah 8:13

Jeremiah 8:13 "I will surely consume them, saith the Lord: there shall be no grapes on the vine, nor figs on the fig tree, and the leaf shall fade; and the things that I have given them shall pass away from them."

Israel had become so insensitive to sin. They had become a perpetual backslider. We find there is this servant of God who looks at all the sin and shares with us how he feels. He reveals to us his innermost feelings as he looks out over God's people.

After they had gone away from God in verse 13 - 22 he says, " I will surely consume them, said the Lord: there shall be no grapes on the vine, nor figs on the fig tree, and the leaf shall fade; and the things that I have given them shall pass away from them. Why do we sit still? Assemble yourselves, and let us enter into the defenced cities, and let us be silent there: for the Lord our God hath put us to silence and given us water of gall to drink, because we have sinned against the Lord. We looked for peace, but no good came; and for a time of health, and behold trouble! The snorting of his horses was heard from Dan: the whole land trembled at the sound of the neighing of his strong ones; for they are come, and have devoured the land, and all that is in it; the city, and those that dwell therein. For, behold, I will send serpents, cockatrices, among you, which will not be charmed, and they shall bite you, saith the Lord. When I would comfort myself against sorrow, my heart is faint in me. Behold the voice of the cry of the daughter of my people because of them that dwell in a far country: Is not the Lord in Zion? Is not her king in her? Why have they provoked me to anger with their graven images, and with strange vanities? The harvest is past, the summer is ended, and we are not saved. For the hurt of the daughter of my people am I hurt; I am black; astonishment hath taken hold on me. Is there no balm in Gilead; is there no physician there? Why then is not the health of the daughter of my people recovered?"

Now turn to the book of Luke. I want you to notice several verses of scripture. And we will skip about a bit. Jesus is baptized and gone into the wilderness. In Luke 4:14 - 28, "And Jesus returned in the power of the Spirit into Galilee; and there went out a fame of him through all the region round about. And he taught in their synagogues, being glorified of all. And he came to Nazareth, where he had been brought up: and, as his custom was, he went into the synagogue on the Sabbath day, and stood up for to read. And there was delivered unto him the book of the prophet Esaias. And when he had opened the book, he found the place where it was written. The spirit of the Lord is upon me, because he hath anointed me to preach the gospel to the poor; he hath sent me to heal the brokenhearted, to preach deliverance to the captives, and recovering of sight to the blind, to set at liberty them that are bruised. To preach the acceptable year of the Lord. And he closed the book and he gave it to again to the minister, and sat down. And the eyes of all them that were in the synagogue were fastened on him. And he began to say unto them, this day is this scripture fulfilled in your ears. And all bare him witness, and wondered at the gracious words which proceeded out of his mouth. And they said, is not this Joseph's son? And he said unto them, ye will surely say unto me this proverb, Physician, heal thyself: whatsoever we have heard done in Capernaum, do also here in thy country. And he said, Verily, I say unto you, No prophet is accepted in his own country. But I tell you of a truth, many widows were in Israel in the days of Elias, when the heaven shut up three years and six months, when great famine was throughout all the land; But unto none of them was Elias sent, save unto Sarepta, a city of Sidon, unto a woman that was a widow. And many lepers were in Israel in the time of Eliseus the prophet; and none of them was cleansed, saving Naaman the Syrian. And all they in the synagogue, when they heard these things, were filled with wrath.

I have tried to feel these past months, as I have prepared this message, the burden of the Lord. And I want you to know; and I am sure you already know it is seriously important to say the things that need to be said. I grew up among you; grew up among people in this community. There is an awful lot in my years, teenage years, that I am not proud of and I am ashamed of. There are some things I wished I had not done. Some things I wished I had not said. There has been something with me ever since I can remember, even as a young boy in Sunday school. There has always been in my heart and in my mind and in my understanding one fact. As strange as it may seem to you, before I was saved and still a sinner by original sin, and before I had committed any actual acts of sin, I knew in my heart that the only life that would ever have any meaning for me was to walk with God. I knew that from my earliest childhood. And as strange as it may seem, when I was committing sin I knew that. When I was doing the very things I knew were wrong, I knew that if my life was to have any meaning, I would have to walk with God.

Not many people can come back home to preach because of their past; too many shady things, too many things people point at and I thank God that in my early years God watched over me and kept me from committing serious immoral or violating immoral purity. I appreciate my wife, who was my girlfriend then, and who helped me in that. God knew there was something he wanted me to do. It made it possible for me to do it in my own hometown, among the people I grew up with. It was when I gave my heart to the Lord; I wanted to be in his service. I wanted to be used for the Lord. I did not know why or where or how God would use me and it took me some time brethren, to understand my calling from God.

You know that most people who are called into what they call full-time service spend most of their praying hours agonizing over God's will for their life. Some of the young people may be saying to yourself, what does God want me to do with my life. Something that will help you and helped me is that God's will for you is exactly the same for me. God is not nearly as impressed with what we do. God is not all impressed whether you are a missionary or a plumber. God's will for your life is found in the Book of Romans. That is we be conformed to the image of his Son. That means every day we live, we become a little more like Jesus. It's God's will for your life and it is God's will for my life. What we do is secondary.

I wanted God to use me and I wanted to know where he wanted me to go and I had some folks helping me to decide what it was God wanted me to do. I settled what God's will for my life was, as far as a location was concerned, many years ago. I settled it in a waiting room at Baptist Hospital about 8 a.m. one Monday morning. I have shared this only three other times and the reason I have not shared this before is because no one understands. It has caused some difficulty in some places when I share this testimony. In that waiting room at Baptist Hospital, God's will for my life became apparent, it became real. God had called me to minister to the body of Christ. He did not call me to be an evangelist, nor a teacher, but God called me to be a shepherd. God called me to give my life for the flock. When I settled that, the burden lifted and I didn't have any trouble anymore with what God wanted me to do. I minister to the body of Christ. That is the burden God put on my heart. I am glad God gives us evangelist, teachers and people with a pastor's heart. I was sitting at Baptist Hospital that Monday morning and one of our teenagers from our church had been in a car accident. She had hit an oak tree that was about six foot through at the base. She hit that tree at about 85 mph with no seatbelt. She was not human looking and every bone in her face was crushed like an eggshell. They had wired the skull to the skin. I sat with that family for 2 days and nights. I was sitting in the waiting room that morning and a young preacher came in and he was all dressed up, freshly shaven and he had on a clean shirt and suit and he walked over to me and said, "I am just wasting my time and I am so sick and tired of this." I asked, "What's the trouble?" His response was "I have got to sit up here while some little girl in my church has her tonsils taken out." I looked him straight in the eye and said, "Brother, you better go back and find out whether God wants you to be a pastor or not." I talked to the same man a few months ago and he is still pastoring a church and still wasting his time he said. God called me and I don't share that much. I shared it the first time to a young student at Bible College, He said, "Brother, if there is anyone who is misguided, you are one of them." He said, "We are saved. The body of Christ is not in danger. It is the world that needs the message. We need to preach the message to those who have never heard it before."

Do you know how I feel about the body of Christ? Do you have any idea the emotions in my heart toward the church and the body of Christ? You see, I grew up not too far from here in the Church of Christ. My folks didn't go to church. I had a little sister about 8 years old. She never missed a Sunday. She would walk out to the highway and catch a ride in the back of a pick-up truck and went to church every Sunday. Every Sunday that little blue-eyed blonde headed sister of mine would go down that gravel road and climb up in the back of that pick-up truck and she would go to Sunday school. Nobody else in the family went and we were all asleep when she left each Sunday. Some of you know that little girl got killed. She got killed waiting for the school bus one morning. All of the sudden, everyone in the family got religion. Everybody started going to church. Oh what a price we paid. Nobody cared whether I was saved or lost. No one ever said they did. When I became a Free Will Baptist and I didn't become a Free Will Baptist because I was pressured. I became a Free Will Baptist because I wanted to, but in the process I lost my family. I lost my mom and dad. I lost my brothers and sisters. I could still go home, but that was about it. No fellowship, nothing but contempt. People told me not worry about it and don't let it bother me. Do you have any idea how much heartache is in that? Do you have any idea how it is to lie in bed at night and weep because you have lost your family because you are trying to serve God the best way you know how? I have said that to say this, I have found in the church, brothers and sisters, moms and dads. I found a love in the church far deeper than I would have ever known. People just don't understand the love I have for the body of Christ.

Jeremiah, in chapter 8, is weeping. He is looking out at the church, God's people and he is crying. There are tears rolling down his cheek and his heart is broken. There is a burden so deep he can't stand it and who is Jeremiah crying over – God's people. It is God's people who have broken his heart and he is crying out after. He is saying what is wrong with God's people. Is there no physician there? Is the king not in Zion? If God is God and if we are his people then why is the hurt of our daughter not healed? Why isn't there victory in the camp of God? I say to you as I look out over God's people, my cry is exactly the same. Is there no physician in her? Is there no balm in Gilead? There is an absence of the shout of victory today among God's people and it hurts me.

Israel had gone out on its own. Each man had gone his own way and did that which was right in his own eyes. They began to worship idols, they seduced the widows and they became more and more wicked until God was grieved in his heart. God didn't say anything to anybody for 430 years. Grieved because of his people and he didn't say anything to anybody. Then suddenly, like a fog lifting on a spring morning, here comes a man out of the wilderness. A strange man dressed in lion's cloth eating locust and wild honey and his message is Repent, Repent. He is talking to God's people. Why? Because God's people had gone away from him and God's people were in trouble and in bondage.

In Luke 4, we find Jesus coming and this strange man out of the wilderness baptizes Jesus in the river Jordan. The spirit comes down upon Jesus in the form of a dove and the Father says this is my beloved Son. Now who is coming to God's people? The physician of Zion is now coming because God's people are in trouble. Whatever you can say about the world and however applicable that is to the world, it is God's people who are in trouble. If you think the world has got troubles, travel from home to home and travel from church to church among God's people. Jesus said himself, I am not sent to the Gentiles, I am sent to the lost sheep of the house of Israel. I am sent to God's people. Why, because God's people are in trouble. Why is God grieved at that? Israel, you see, was God's own people. Israel was to be an objective witness. Israel was to be the evangelistic center of the universe. Israel was to be a blueprint, a model of a redeemed community of people. God wanted Israel to be an objective witness for all the Gentiles around. To look at Israel and say look how healthy those people are and look at the joy those people have. Look at that husband and wife, look at those children. We need that and that is what God wanted Israel to be to the rest of the world.

But you see, they could talk about God and could read their Old Testament and even witness to the Gentiles I'm sure. The Gentiles were looking and saw God's people in big trouble. What we see and hear are two different things. Have you ever gone to a health food store? That has become a big rage now days. If you eat enough alfalfa sprouts you not only chase rabbits but you can catch them. You walk through the health food store and find stuff that will make you a Charles Atlas type. You will find things that are good for you blood and circulation, hair, complexion, etc. If you take all of that you will be a perfect specimen. Have you ever noticed the clerks that work in the health food store? Some look like they have been in the grave for 4 days: hollow-eyed, pale, coughing and you say if I buy that will it do for me what it did for you? Yes sir; well I don't want any. You see he is telling you all about health food, but you are seeing something totally different.

Many times Christians go witnessing with a long face. They say, don't you want to become a Christian, in a dry monotone voice. Or you are standing out front of the church and with a sad expression and tone in your voice, you say, "We want to welcome you to our church today." And the visitor or the person you are witnessing to say, if I become a Christian will it do for me what it has done for you? Yes; then I don't want any of it. Folks can tell you about God and about the things of God, but we see something else. God wanted Israel to be an objective witness and he wants you and I to be an objective witness. That is what the body of Christ is all about. The body of Christ should be a community of redeemed men and women in a certain location living differently from everybody else. Do you know why we have lost our power? There is no difference. If you go to the same places, if you do the same things, if you say the same things, why do they want to be a Christian? They can do the same things you do and they don't have to tithe. Sort of like the difference between an alcoholic and a drunk. A drunk doesn't have to pay dues, the alcoholic does.

In Jeremiah, his face is wet from weeping. He is burdened for the hurt of his people and he says, "Is there no king in her? Where is the king of Israel, is there no balm in Gilead?" You see God's people had sold themselves into bondage. In Luke 4 the Lord Jesus comes and he is filled with the spirit and begins to work his miracles. And this verse I love and let me change it a little bit just for me. 'And he came to Ashland City where he had been brought up.' That is not really what it says, it says" and he came to Nazareth where he had been brought up."

Do you know what an expert is? An expert is anybody out of town with a briefcase. There is nothing like going home to minister. You see the cartoon in the paper about the marriage counselor and he had the man and wife in the office. He is counseling with them and he is on the phone. He says, yes dear, yes dear, no dear, yes dear, sure I will dear." You know it is possible to counsel people in their marriage and your own marriage fall apart? Did you know that? You can deal with other people's children and your own children become rebels. I have seen it happen. I will never forget a little girl sitting out under a cedar tree at camp one year. She was about 11 years old. She was sitting under the tree crying. We began to talk and her father was one of the most respected ministers in the area. An evangelist, who stayed busy all the time and that little girl's heart was broken and was weeping her eyes out. She said that her daddy didn't love her anymore. He never spent time with the family anymore. She said before he got saved and started preaching, we had fun together and now he doesn't have time for me.

Have you ever seen the sign that says, "God first, others second, me last"? You may think that is humility brother, but it is stupidity. Your first responsibility is your own spiritual condition between you and God, but your second responsibility is to your family and third responsibility is to the church, not the other way around. I ministered to a young fellow one night who was a Bible College student, married and had children. He was going to school, take the exams, working part-time, visiting and witnessing. His wife had already come to me with a broken heart. She would lay awake at night and cry all night long. He came to me and said, "Brother, I want to talk to you and I want to do it in love", he said, "We are not doing enough for the Lord. I believe the lights of the church should be on six nights a week." My reply was, "Brother, there is something wrong with a man that can't go home. "He was worried about everybody's wife and children but his own. You can do that you know and lose your own family.

God has a cure for that and it is called sending you home. When I got saved and answered the call to preach I told the Lord I would go anywhere he wanted me to go. That's right, he sent me to Ashland City, and he sent me home where people knew me all my life. He sent me home. Remember the maniac that was saved and healed from his demonic condition? He said God; I will go wherever you want me to go. I'll carry the gospel; I'll do anything you will have me to do. Jesus said to him, go home. You know why God sends us home? It is the most difficult place to demonstrate what God has done to you and for you through Jesus Christ. It is much easier to go to another city or state. The most difficult place is in the home, in your office, in your church or wherever God has placed you as an objective witness.

The physician is come and he opens the word and he began to read from Isaiah. Who is he reading to – God's people. He is not out in the bar. He is not in the marketplace, but he is in the church and he is with God's people. He is with those people who love God and who are serving God the best they know how. To the best light and the best knowledge they have, they are trying to do what God wants them to do. That is who Jesus is talking to. There is joy of preaching where they don't know you and the joy of preaching where they never heard before. But going home where people have been preached to all their lives and some fellow, who grew up in the community, dares to preach to you and your say, I've heard that all my life and they just turn it off is difficult. It is difficult especially when there is depression, conflicts and problems. I have a lady in my church that never brags on my preaching. She is a throne in my flesh. She will go visit another church somewhere and come back the next Sunday and say, Brother Boyd, you should have heard that young fellow preach last Sunday. I would say, under my breath, I preached the same way and she didn't carry on that way. Your preacher can get up, preach on discipline and discipleship and all of you yawn and go to sleep. You can hear the same message on the PTL club and you want to call and tell everyone about it.

The apostle Paul said one time some interesting words and I stumbled by this by mistake. He said, "I am an apostle of Jesus Christ by faith to you that believe." But Paul said, "I am an apostle". That is, I can minister to you, if you believe I can minister to you. Do you know something that could revolutionize our church? If every Sunday school teacher could walk before their classes and have every student in their class have the Holy Spirit quicken in their hearts and say here is a teacher sent from God. You see, I am a teacher if you believe me to be a teacher. I am a minister if you believe me to be a minister. Jesus was the Son of God, but there were some to whom he was not the Son of God. They didn't believe him. A pastor can come to the pulpit or a Sunday school teacher can walk before his or her class and something in your heart is quickened and says here is a man or woman from God. Faith leaps up in your heart and faith leaps up in his or her heart. There is communication in spiritual things. Paul said the Lord hath anointed me to preach the gospel to the poor. Who are the poor? Somebody said that is everybody that is broke and living on the American Express card. No, that is not what he is talking about. God has anointed me to preach the gospel to those who are conscious of their need.

How many of us are conscious of our spiritual need? Have you ever, during the day, let that temper get the best of you? You say something unkind, you have some thought and then that night you go to pray to the Lord and the Lord whispers to you, "I know thy works. You begin to search your heart and say God it is true. In my heart there is envy and jealousy and all those other things that Paul lists in Ephesians. How many of us are conscious of our spiritual needs? That is the poor. The Bible says he hath filled the poor with good things, the rich he sent away empty. What does it mean to preach the acceptable year of the Lord? People in biblical days could sell themselves when they got so far in debt. They could sell themselves for 7 years and after 7 years by law, they had to be set free. It was a great time of being reunited with their families and was call the year of jubilee. The acceptable year and Jesus says I come in the jubilee I come to set the captives free. That is exactly what he did – he healed the broken hearted. Want to ask you church, have you experienced a broken heart? Do you know what it is like to have a broken heart? I realized 15 years ago that every time I got in the pulpit there was a broken heart on every pew. We come to church and we've got our faces on and smiling from ear to ear and our hearts are broken. Our spirits are wounded. That may be in the world, but I am concerned today about the broken hearts in God's house. I have seen men and women whose spouses left them. I have seen a home where a child has died. I've seen a place where friends had proven to be an enemy. I have listened to these people and I have ministered with those people and they say they are broken inside. My spirit is broken, I'm wounded and I'm hurt. Someone comes up and puts their arm around you and your heart is breaking, your spirit is wounded and they say, brother what you need to do is pray more. That's good advice, but it will not heal a broken heart.

I want to tell you there are folks in our community that have been from church to church trying to seek God and tried to fellowship with God's people and have gone away feeling there is nothing anywhere. Can you believe that there are folks in this community, who have been to this church, looked at it, tried to fellowship with God's people and have gone away broken-hearted, back-sliding in their heart walking away from God.

Jesus is the only physician I know that can heal a broken heart. "I have come to preach deliverance to the captives," he said. These were spiritual prisoners of war. These were those who had gone out unprepared to meet the enemy and found themselves trapped, bound up and enslaved. They were unprepared to fight the devil. In Vietnam we had a lot of good men taken prisoner. Taken as slaves, you might say, bound up and put into prisons. And folks, they were still citizens of the United States of America. We get folks in our church, we get them to come to the altar, and we pray with them, they accept Christ as their Savior. They go outside this door, they go out to fight the devil, but they are not prepared to fight the devil and found themselves entrapped and bound up. They found themselves enslaved and they came back to us and we tell them we knew you wouldn't make it, we knew you wouldn't hold out. We stepped on them and pushed them a little further down. That's happened, when someone should have taken the sword of the Spirit and cut that captive free.

Preach to the blind – those who have been in darkness so long they couldn't see correctly any longer. You know what that means to me? It means to be hurt by others of God's people. This is very precious to me and very serious. I want to ask you a question. Who can hurt you the most? Isn't it the one that you love the most? The world can't hurt you. The world can't hurt me. But a lot of God's people have been hurt by God's little helpers-the sheriffs of the kingdom of God who are always defending God and who are going to keep you from doing this or that. They are defending God all the time and don't care how it hurts.

When I pastored a church in Nashville, I preached on Wednesday night for seven weeks on love. The final night of that series of lessons, God showed me that he's got a real sense of humor. Walking in the back door of the church was a hippie. He had been a local boy, but had gone away and was back in town. He walked in that night wearing a Budweiser t-shirt, roman sandals, and hair down to his waist and stunk to high heaven. He proceeded to walk to the front row and sit down. You don't think God has a sense of humor? I had been preaching on love for 7 weeks and here he sits. What I wanted to do was, 'let's have a business meeting, form a committee and see what we are going to do with this fellow", but we didn't. We held our nose and hugged him. He got saved, baptized and went off to a bible college in another city. People can be hurt in the church more deeply than anywhere else in the world. People in the church have feelings different from those in the world and we ought to recognize their feelings.

Luke 4:20 says, "And he closed the book, and he gave it again to the minister, and sat down. And the eyes of all them that were in the synagogue were fastened on him. That means it became very, very quiet in that place. Remember what He said. It is all about God coming to his people. God through his Son the Lord Jesus Christ reaching out to bind up those who are bruised, broken-hearted, captive and blind; to set free those who are lost.

There will come a time of invitation, a time of decision and you will say I know that's true; my heart is breaking and my spirit is overwhelmed and I have got this and that problem. I know that I can be free and that Jesus Christ can save me from my sin and heal my broken heart. But Satan will say to you "who is this?" just as they said of Jesus. Who is this, isn't this Joseph's son? Who is this fellow preaching to us? Didn't we know his father? Didn't he grow up around here?

Some of you may say I knew Terry Boyd when he rode the mule through his mother's house. It doesn't have anything to do with me. A prophet hath no honor in his own country. Remember what they said to Jesus on that day, physician heal thyself. Jesus said if you don't want me to minister to you that is alright, but remember there were many widows in Israel, but God only sent Elisha to one. Only one was saved. There were many lepers in Israel, but only one was saved and his name was Naaman. Oh Jerusalem, Jerusalem how often would I gather thee as a hen doeth her chicks, but you would not.

I say to you church, Oh church the spirit of God is here. The moment of decision has come. The Bible says Jesus left the synagogue and as he walked along a man possessed of the devil cried out, "God have mercy on me". Jesus said, that is why I came. Jesus wants you to do two things. First he wants to be your physician. He wants to reach down in that heart and heal that broken heart. He wants to reach down and cleanse you of your sin. He wants to save your soul. Secondly, he wants you to carry the physician to others. The king is here; the physician is here; the balm of Gilead is here. The law of the Spirit is here. God is coming to his people and God can meet any need you have. I pray that we feel the touch of the physician in our hearts. Lord, help us to bring that spiritual need we have to you that it might be healed.

Prayer: Father, we bow before you realizing that in this message we have shared personal thoughts. I believe that you have been pleased with us in what we shared because you placed it in my heart. I remember the time when I sat in a church like this and my heart was broken. Lord, I remember that time when I almost gave up preaching. I was making preparation to leave the ministry. I talked to a Christian and was hurt even more; and you came and ministered and healed my broken heart. Father, if there is one here tonight who has been hurt by one of God's people and been bruised, the physician is here tonight. Lord reach out and minister to that heart. There may be one here who has, in their heart, some feeling towards another child of God. Maybe not in this church but there is something hindering them. You have come to heal it and put it away. There may be one who does not know you as their personal Savior and you have come Father as Savior. Help them to come and receive you. Father, this time is giving you the opportunity to come and minister to your people. And as we wait in these final moments, I pray that we would feel the touch of the physician in our hearts. Help us bring that spiritual need we have to you that it might be healed. We will wait before you in faith believing in the name of Jesus. Amen.

WITH *the* WORD

15

Behold the Man

John 19:1-6

"Then Pilate therefore took Jesus, and scourged him. And the soldiers plaited a crown of thorns, and put it on his head, and they put on him a purple robe, and said, Hail, King of the Jews! And they smote him with their hands. Pilate therefore went forth again, and saith unto them, Behold, I bring him forth to you, that ye may know that I find no fault in him. Then came Jesus forth, wearing the crown of thorns, and the purple robe. And Pilate saith unto them, Behold the man! When the chief priests therefore and officers saw him, they cried out, saying, crucify him, crucify him. Pilate saith unto them, Take ye him, and crucify him: for I find no fault in him."

I suppose there is something about all of our natural curiosity. All of us have some desire to see and meet people who have become famous or made a name for themselves in society. If the president were to come to our community, I am sure there would be a number of people to come and see him. We just have a curiosity about folks who have made a name for themselves. I believe as a preacher of the gospel of the Lord Jesus Christ that on any given Sunday morning we should be just as eager to see the greatest man who ever lived – the God man, the Lord Jesus Christ. I believe we ought to say, as those people said to the disciples, "We would see Jesus". I think we ought to demand to see him in our singing and in the preaching. We ought to see

Jesus in the lives of our separate members of every congregation. We ought to see Jesus.

In the text I chose we find that Pilate had taken the Lord Jesus Christ and had scourged him. Now before this scourging had taken place he had been subjected to all kinds of inhuman cruelties. He had been spat upon, he had been insulted, all kinds of open shame that our Lord had been put through. I can see in this scripture, as Pilate comes forth to the balcony of his dwelling place down beneath in the courtyard there is a great multitude of people who have gathered to see what's going to happen to this Jesus. Pilate comes forth and raises his hands to get the multitude to get quite. When he has gotten their attention, Jesus comes forth to stand beside Pilate. There Pilate stands beside the Son of God. He stands beside that one that so loved us, he was willing to endure that which he is enduring. Pilate got the people's attention and as Jesus is presented before them Pilate turns to Jesus and to the multitude and says, "Behold the man". From that great multitude of people came the cry, crucify him, crucify him! Pilate said you take him and crucify him, but let it be known that I personally find no fault in him.

Today I, as the preacher, want to take the role of Pilate. I want to stand before you in this pulpit and say to every one of you gathered here, "Behold the man". Behold Jesus of Nazareth, look upon him. I want you to see the man who was wounded for your transgressions; bruised for our iniquities; who bore our grief and carried our sorrows and who was crucified in our stead. I want you to see him. Behold the man as that multitude did.

Do you ever get tired of the preacher talking about Jesus? If I continue in the way I'm going by teaching Sunday school in the morning, preaching Sunday morning and night and Wednesday evening service, do you realize how many times a week that I preach? Do you ever get tired of hearing about Jesus? We talk about Jesus Christ in the manager, on the cross, in the tomb, his ministry and say the same things over and over about Jesus, don't we. Do you ever get tired of hearing about him? I had rather hear someone say the same thing over and over about Jesus than to hear something new about someone else, wouldn't you?

You can never get enough of Jesus. Jesus is the theme every preacher must have. He is the heart of every message. If you take Jesus out of the sermon, you take the heart out of it. A priceless sermon is a joy to hell and the sorrow to heaven. There is but one theme and that is Jesus. You can never hear too much about Jesus. Whether you preach Christ in prophesy, Christ in the manger, Christ on the cross, Christ in the tomb, Christ in his resurrection, Christ in his ascension, Christ in his intersession, Christ in his coming again, you can never hear too much of Jesus Christ. Every message has to center in the person of the Lord Jesus Christ.

If I were to stand before you and were to preach a message to you that did not center in the Lord Jesus Christ, I would be wasting your time and endangering the souls of many. Therefore, behold the man. Behold that Jesus we have talked about every Sunday and Sunday night, every Wednesday night and every Sunday in Sunday school. Behold him again as he stands before you. If you behold Jesus rightly today, if you see him in the right way, there are many things that you will profit. For example, if you behold the Christ of Calvary, you will receive knowledge and learn something that you can learn nowhere else, except at the cross. There are some lessons taught there that are not taught anywhere else. Only there can you learn the tremendous lessons that God intends for us to learn. At the cross, when we behold Jesus, we learn the nature of sin. All of us have seen a thousand pictures of sin. When you think of the Garden of Eden when it was a place of beauty and then you behold the Garden of Eden now and see it barren and desolate, sin did that. When you behold Adam and Eve, as that heavenly couple and see them digging in the sand trying to dig out a living, sin did that. Over and over again there are pictures in the word of God that teach us what sin is like.

When I read in the book of Genesis about the flood that covered this earth, and when my mind begins to comprehend what took place when God destroyed the earth. I see women and children shrieking in horror as they are carried away by the watery tomb. The cry comes back to me that sin did that. When I see Sodom and Gomorrah, those two cities that are literally covered in fire and brimstone, sin did that. But it is only when we see the cross and see God's only begotten Son dying upon that cross, spilling his blood as an innocent sacrifice do we really see and learn the lesson of the nature of sin.

How God must have hated sin. What was it that brought all the sickness into this world? Sin. What was it that brought that horrible thing of death that snatches our loved ones away? What brought that into this world? Sin did that. What was it that built hell and the regions of the damned? Sin did. But of all the pictures that we can imagine none can give us a more accurate picture than the worst thing sin did. When it took the Son of God and nailed him on the cross, our sin fashioned the cross. It was our sin that drove the nails; it was our sin that put the spear in his side; it was our sin that pushed that crown of thorns down upon his brow. Sin did all of that.

We learn also, when we look at the cross, the sureness of God's justice. Why does God demand a sacrifice? Why, if God can do all things, did he demand that a penalty be made for sin? Why didn't he find some other way to deal with Adam and Eve except to penalize them and the whole human race with sin and the penalty of it? Why didn't God find some other way? The reason is because God is just. God is a judge who is just. Just as any true judge cannot look at a man, who commits a crime, and say this crime means nothing, I'll let you go; neither can God, who is a just judge, look upon sin and say it is nothing. As a just God, he must demand that every sin be punished. He must demand that every sin receive the proper punishment and wages. The scripture says," the soul that sinneth shall die. The wages of sin is death, but the gift of God is eternal life through Jesus Christ our Lord," Romans 6:23.

So in being just, the penalty of sin must fall upon the sinner or it must fall upon someone else. The scripture says that, "God so loved the world that he gave his only begotten Son that whosoever believeth in him should not perish but have everlasting life", John 3:16. Jesus said, let it fall upon me. Just as they were singing, I should have been crucified, I was guilty I had no way to answer, there were coming to carry me away and someone said, I'll take his place. I'll die in his stead. That is exactly the way it happened. So we learn something about the justice of God.

The scripture in Romans 8:32 tells us, "He that spared not his own Son but delivered him up for us all, how shall he not with him also freely give us all things." You see Jesus had no sin. Jesus was spotless. He was absolutely pure. He was beyond sin and when he went to the cross, the sin that was upon him was imputed sin. It was your sin and my sin. Our sins are actual sins. I am guilty of mine and you are guilty of yours. Jesus had no sin of his own. If God punished imputed sin by the death of his Son, how much more then will he punish actual sin? If God spared not his own Son, whose sin was imputed sin, we ask ourselves the question of Hebrews 2:3, "How shall we escape if we neglect so great salvation."

If there is no one to bear our sin we must bear it. God's justice will be carried out. So we learn of the nature of sin, the sureness of God's justice and we learn a tremendous lesson about God's love. The whole world is an expression of God's love. Did you know that? The whole world, we are living in, is an expression of God's love. If we know how to interpret and if we knew how to read it, everything we see and behold is an expression of God's love. If you were to gather all the flowers together they would say God is love. Even the storms speak a language and if we knew how to interpret it would spell God is love. Everything about us spells of love. But to understand God's love, to understand how deeply God loved the world, we don't look at a daisy painted on the back of a car, or some other kind of superficial expression of human love. The only way we can fully understand God's love is to behold the man; to behold the Lord, to behold the Christ of Calvary.

God so loved us he gave his only begotten Son to climb that hill of Calvary and to endure what he endured because he loved us. When we behold the man we learn something about emotions. Did you ever go to a play or even a church service for that matter and just look at the people in the audience and see in their expression their emotions? For example, most of the time when you come to church you look around and see on people's face boredom. One preacher said one morning in his announcements, "we are going to have an official board meeting tonight." That night 14 people showed up. He asked one gentlemen why he was there because he was not on the board. He replied, "Well, you said you had a board meeting and I was bored stiff. If anybody qualified for a board meeting, I'm one of them." You can see on their faces the expression of you. You can see on folk's faces the expression of sorrow and the expression of boredom. The emotions of the heart are registered on their face.

When you look at the cross and behold the Lord of Calvary, what should our feelings be? What should respond from us when looking at Jesus, to beholding him? We should feel sorrowful, we should feel sorrow for sin. The whole world wants to be happy. We want to be happy at the expense of anything or anybody. We must find some kind of happiness. The whole world is in a chase to become happy. But there is a time to be sorrowful. There is a time to feel sorrow for our sins. There's a time when we look at our puny lives and look at what the Lord of Glory did for us and weep at the feet of Jesus over our sin. There is a time to cry. That time to weep is when we are convicted of our sin. When we behold the Lord of Glory, we ought to feel that sorrow in our heart for sin and that sorrow will cause us to repent and confess.

If you have never known penitential sorrow, then you have never known spiritual joy. Whatever you've experienced is something else, but it is not spiritual joy. If you have not at one time wept in your heart; if you have not felt your spirit crushed because of the weight of conviction of sin then you have never in your life experienced any kind of spiritual joy. Because God breaks you before he makes you. There is a time to be sorrowful and it is when we behold the Lord of glory. I wish all of us could weep over our sin. If we, today, could fall at the feet of Jesus and weep over our failures; to weep because of how we've let the Lord of glory down; how we have sinned and come short of the glory of God.

Do you remember when you were first converted; how you wept over your sin? Do you remember how you wept when you came to Jesus and he took that burden off your back? How long has it been since you felt that same kind of burden? Sometimes we get hardened to it. We need to probe our hearts and search our hearts and then come to the feet of Jesus. I am reminded of the words, "Alias and did my Savior bleed and did my sovereign die, would he devote that sacred head for such a worm as I." Did my sin kill the Lord of glory? Did he devote that sacred head for such a worm as I? Did I slay the Lord of glory? Did my sin nail him to the cross? Yes it did. But drops of grief can never repay the debt of love I owe. We ought to view his death with sorrow and say here Lord I give myself away tis all that I can do.

To behold the man means we ought to make some holy resolutions. Every pastor that I know is concerned over his people. Every pastor I know is concerned over the people in his congregation who are not walking close to the Lord. He is concerned about those who have made a profession of faith and yet given no expression to it. They are not living for the Lord. If I could get my entire congregation, along with myself, to behold the man rightly; if we could see him correctly we would say to the world, you have no attraction for me. The world would lose its attraction to all of us if we could behold the man rightly today.

The lost person should give himself to Jesus. There is salvation only in him and you can look to him and live. I want to present, as Pilate did, him to you and I want a response from you. I am going to ask you to do something. I want you to imagine in your eyes and in your heart that Jesus stands beside me today as he stood beside Pilate that day. I am going to say to you right now, "Behold the Lord of Glory!" Behold the man! Look at him! View that one who was wounded for you that was bruised for you and carried your sorrow and your grief. Behold him today! If there is anyone who does not believe that Jesus was who he claimed to be; if you believe that Jesus was an imposter and a deceiver I want you to raise your hand right now. If there is anyone who believes he was not what he claimed to be, honest enough to raise your hand. If you believe that he had all authority in heaven and in earth and if you believe that he was the Son of God sent as the Savior for the world, I want you to stand right where you are. You have looked and beheld him and believe that he is exactly what he claimed to be. Behold the Man!

Prayer: Our heavenly father we thank you for your great love to us. We thank you that while we were astray going our own way and while we were yet sinners you sent your Son to come into the world to die for us. Because of that death on the cross, we have access to the throne of God. Father, we thank you for all the possibilities involved in salvation. We thank you for the new creature, the new creation that is possible through coming to the Lord Jesus Christ. We thank you for your promise of coming again. We realize from time to time we forget that great promise and we live as though you could not come at any moment. We know when we study the scripture that your coming could be at any moment. Help us to let that truth get down into our very being. Help us to be gripped by the fact that you could come at any time and seeing that help us to change our lives. Father we pray that most of all, during this time we wait for your returning that we would heed your command to occupy till you come. Help us to be concerned for lost souls and to weep over those who are lost. May we witness to those who need the Lord and cooperate with the ministry of the church in reaching lost souls. Our prayer is that you not come and catch us unprepared. Help us to watch and be ready and have many with us when you return. I pray that if there is one who is not ready for the sudden return of the Lord that the Holy Spirit will speak to that heart. I pray if there is a Christian who needs to get some things straightened out in their lives waiting for the Lord that they will do so now. If there is one who does not know you as their personal Savior, I pray that they will accept you today. Have your own way in our hearts and we will praise you for all that is done. In Jesus' name. Amen

16

A Portrait of Jesus

Isaiah 53

The greatest song that could be written would be a song about the Lord Jesus Christ and the greatest poem ever written would be about the Lord Jesus Christ. The greatest portrait every painted would be of our Lord Jesus Christ. I wish photography had been developed in the days of Jesus. I wish I had a picture of Him. I wish I knew what Jesus looks like. We do not have a photo, but we have a word picture, the greatest portrait of our Lord is given to us by Isaiah. Isaiah prophesied what Jesus would like, what he would be wearing, how he would be treated and how he would look when he went to the cross to purchase your salvation and mine. Let's read this word portrait of our Lord and Savior Jesus Christ as painted by Isaiah.

Isaiah 53:1-12 "Who hath believed our report? And to whom is the arm of the Lord revealed? For he shall grow up before him as a tender plant, and as a root out of a dry ground: he hath no form nor comeliness; and when we shall see him, there is no beauty that we should desire him. He is despised and rejected of men; a man of sorrows, and acquainted with grief: and we hid as it were our faces from him; he was despised and we esteemed him not. Surely he hath borne our griefs, and carried our sorrows: yet we did esteem him stricken, smitten of God, and afflicted. But he was wounded for our transgressions; he was bruised for our iniquities: the chastisement of our peace was upon him; and with his stripes we are healed. All we like sheep have gone astray; we have turned everyone to his own way; and the Lord hath laid on him the iniquity of us all. He was oppressed, and he was afflicted, but he opened not his mouth: he is brought as a lamb to the slaughter, and as a sheep before her shearers is dumb, so he openeth not his mouth. He was taken from prison and from judgment: and who shall declare his generation? For he was cut off out of the land of the living: for the transgression of my people was he stricken. And he made his grave with the wicked, and with the rich in his death; because he had done no violence neither was any deceit in his mouth. Yet it pleased the Lord to bruise him; he hath put him to grief: when thou shalt make his soul an offering for sin, he shall see his seed, he shall prolong his days, and the pleasure of the Lord shall prosper in his hand. He shall see of the travail of his soul, and shall be satisfied: by his knowledge shall my righteous servant justify many; for he shall bear their iniquities. Therefore will I divide the spoil with the strong; because he hath poured out his soul unto death: and he was numbered with the transgressors; and he bare the sin of many, and made intercession for the transgressors".

Jesus was a man not of beauty that we see in pictures painted, not a well groomed man. But when Jesus went to the cross he was a pitiful sight. He was a man who was beaten until his face had no resemblance of a human being, you could not tell if he was a man or beast. His flesh had been torn from his back with a whip and above all of that there was sorrow and grief from an inner experience. A man who had no beauty that we would look upon and we hid our faces when we saw him on the cross because of the terrible way he had been treated by man. As I go back just a little bit after reading Isaiah, I see our Lord Jesus Christ being led like a criminal to a whipping post. I see him as they tie his hands behind his back and tie him to a stake with his feet barely touching the ground. I see the biggest and strongest Roman soldier come down upon the body of our Lord time and time again with that cat of nine tails which has a piece of metal at the end of each strip which fastened on the body like fish hooks and when the whip was drawn back, it tore pieces of flesh from his body. The whipping Jesus received was illegal, no man could receive 40 strips, but Pilate intended for the strips to take the place of crucifixion. He thought that surely when people saw our Lord being beaten to the point of death they would no longer cry out for the crucifixion. But the beating only proved to be a prelude to the crucifixion, making it more sorrowful for him and made his suffering more when he did go to the cross. The servants came and washed away the blood, but they could not wash away the guilt of those that had put the stripes across his back. Pilate would come and say, "I wash my hands of innocent blood", but he could not do away with the guilt. He could not do away with the stain. To me, the prophesy of Isaiah concerning the crucifixion of our Lord, is the most precious prophesy in the Old Testament.

In recent months, I have heard this verse, "He was wounded for our transgressions, he was bruised for our iniquities: the chastisement of our peace was upon him; and with his stripes we are healed." I have heard that passage of scripture taken out of context. I have heard that passage being polluted to lose its meaning. The most precious thing in all the world to the child of God and to the world itself, is the shed blood of our Lord and Savior Jesus Christ. And Satan knows how precious that is to all of us and he would have us to pollute it until the blood of Jesus has no meaning. Why was Jesus striped? Why did he endure the chastisement of our peace? It has been taken out of context to mean God never intended for anybody to be sick. For the scripture says, "...by his stripes we are healed" and I have had that passage of scripture used to me when I was sick or when I had an infirmity of the body. That scripture was quoted to me and said that by Jesus crucifixion you are healed. God does not intend for you to be sick. People take that verse of scripture and say God has already bought your health so pray and claim Isaiah 53:5. So you pray it, claim it and don't get well and they say you have already got your healing. It's yours you just don't have the faith to make it a reality in your heart. I have heard that until I am sick of hearing it. Why was Jesus striped? Why was he chastised? Chastisement refers to punishment. It infers guilt. Did Jesus deserve to be whipped? A thousand times NO! Jesus never did anything except good. Every miracle Jesus performed was for someone else's benefit. He walked among those who were lame and healed them. He walked among those who were blind and gave them sight. He walked among those who were deaf and gave them their hearing. He even raised the dead to live again. But his miracles were not for his own benefit. He was one man the world could say went around doing good. He didn't deserve to be whipped. He was beaten unmercifully and the stripes were laid upon him and blood was shed for your sin and for mine. As we watch that soldier take that whip and come down upon the back of our Lord, we see our sin being put upon him. We see the sin of the world put upon the back of our Lord Jesus Christ. The scripture says that was our sin put on him. For all have sinned and come short of the glory of God. There is none righteous, no not one. The soul that sinneth shall die. And then in Isaiah 53:6 says "All we like sheep have gone astray; we have turned everyone to his own way; and the Lord hath laid on him the iniquity of us all". Our sins were laid upon him. God looked down from heaven and saw man in his sin and God being an honest, righteous and holy judge had no other alternative but to punish sin. So he looked for someone who could be a substitute for man's sin. The legend is that Moses came to God and said let me go down and die for the sin of the world. God said Moses there is sin in your life. David, a man after God's own heart, asked God to let him go, but there was sin in his life. And Jesus came to his father and said let me go. And all the host of heaven cried out No not the son of glory. Jesus said, Greater love hath no man than to lay down his life for a friend. Jesus sped past planets, the sun, the moon and the stars and came and shed his blood. Hebrews 9:22 says: "… without shedding of blood is no remission". There is no remission of sin. From the time God placed the blood on the doorpost in every house in Egypt who believe, until the blood was shed upon the cross of Calvary, we see that salvation came only through the shed blood of some innocent substitute. In every incident, salvation was purchased by an innocent substitute shedding his blood for the guilty. That is why we read: "… by his stripes we are healed." Not that we might have a cure for arthritis, not that you might not have a sinus headache, but because your soul is sick. As the psalmist cried out in Psalm 41:4, "Have mercy on me, O God and heal my soul for I have sinned against thee". Chastisement means someone is guilty and they are being corrected like a father. Jesus was not guilty. But the scripture says he took upon himself the chastisement of our peace.

Hebrews 2:14 reads, "Forasmuch then as the children are partakers of flesh and blood, he also himself likewise took part of the same; that through death he might destroy him that had the power of death, that is, the devil". Romans 5:1, "Therefore being justified by faith, we have peace with God through our Lord Jesus Christ". Ephesians 2:14 – 17 "For he is our peace, who hath made both one, and hath broken down the middle wall of partition between us; Having abolished in his flesh the enmity, even the law of commandments contained in ordinances; for to make in himself of twain one new man, so making peace; And that he might reconcile both unto God in one body by the cross, having slain the enmity thereby: and came and preached peace to you which were afar off and to them that were nigh." Jesus came and endured the suffering because our souls were sick and dying. Our souls were condemned to hell and Jesus came and endured the stripes which was our sin that we might be reconciled again with God and have peace with God. The scripture says, therefore being justified by faith, we have peace with God through our Lord and Savior Jesus Christ. Those stripes mean salvation. Men are lost and the remedy for lost men is the shed blood of Christ. The scripture says that the blood of his Son cleanses us from all unrighteousness. Isaiah said come now and let us reason together, saith the Lord, though your sins be as scarlet, they shall be as snow. And though they be like crimson, they shall be as wool. You know there is a lot of difference between scarlet and snow. Jesus makes the difference between crimson and snow white.

How does God look at our sin? How can God take our sin which is red like crimson and make it white as snow? Ladies, the next time you put a red tablecloth on your table take a red glass out of your cabinet and look at that red tablecloth through a red glass and it will be white. A red cloth looked at through a red glass appears white. When Jesus Christ came and shed his rich royal blood for our sins, God looked at our sin through that blood and it was white as snow. Those stripes mean heaven. John 3: 14-15 says, " And as Moses lifted up the serpent in the wilderness, even so must the Son of man be lifted up; That whosoever believeth in him should not perish, but have eternal life." Imagine Moses placing a serpent on a pole outside the camp and people were being bitten and dying and Moses came to those people and said look and live. Turn your eyes upon the brazen serpent and you will live. Jesus was lifted up and every prophet of God and every preacher since, who knew God, and had an understanding of the word of God have told people by the thousands, look and live. As Moses lifted up the serpent in the wilderness that they might be healed, so God has lifted up his own Son. If you would look upon him in faith believing, you would be saved. Those stripes mean salvation. Those stripes mean that a soul can be healed. Those stripes mean heaven. Does the world appreciate the stripes of Jesus? Is it not true that every day, multitudes of people live as if God had no meaning in their life – as though God had no place in their life? They go everyday trampling upon the blood of Jesus Christ that was shed for them yet they will not accept it. What about the Christian? Does the child of God really appreciate what Jesus went through to purchase our salvation? Do we appreciate the suffering, the untold pain of physical and emotional strain? The blood of the stripes was the only blood ever drawn from the body of Jesus by the hand of man. The scripture says at the last supper, Jesus took the wine and said this is the blood which is shed for you, yet his blood was still in his body. The scripture also says that when he went into the garden he prayed as if it were great drops of blood, but it was from an inner experience. When they striped him, it was blood drawn by the hand of man. Do we appreciate that? Do we appreciate the amount of suffering Jesus went through for us? Do we appreciate the fact that Jesus had to say, "My God, my God why hast thou forsaken me"? If the child of God appreciated what Jesus did for them, we would not have to beg them to serve him. You would not have to plead with the child of God to become active for God. You would not have to plead with the child of God to go to church. I believe that Jesus Christ could endure much more the pain, the suffering and agony of Calvary than he can the indifference on the part of people today. When Jesus came to Golgotha, they hanged him on a tree, they drove great nails through his hands and feet and made a Calvary. They crowned him with a crown of thorns; red were his wounds and deep. For those were cruel and crude days and human flesh was cheap. But when Jesus came to America, they simply passed him by. They never touched a hand of his they just let him die. For man had grown more tender, they would not have caused him pain. They would just walk down the street and left him in the rain. Still Jesus prayed, Father, forgive them for they know not what they do and still it rained the winter rain that drenched him through and through. The crowd went home and left the streets without a soul to see. And Jesus crouched against the wall and prayed for Calvary. Oh Father, let me endure the pain and the suffering, the shame and the spitting, hitting and whipping. God don't subject me to indifference. Don't subject me to be ignored; I had rather die on Calvary. Must Jesus bear the cross along and all the world go free? No there is a cross for every man and there is a cross for me.

Prayer: Our heavenly Father as we think about the rich, royal blood of our Lord and Savior Jesus Christ staining an old cruel cross and we see that blood drip down upon his lower garment and onto the pavement below, we realize the agony that he endured, the emotional strain, the forsakenness of God. Our hearts are broken and our hearts realize that all of that was for me. Greater love hath no man than to lay down his life for a friend. Father, help us not to look at that cross in all of its shame and turn around and say I don't care. God help us not to be indifferent, but help us to appreciate all that Jesus did on the cross. Help us to take him down from the cross and wipe his wounds and tenderly place him in our hearts. Father, I pray that the Holy Spirit would take up where we quit and do what we cannot do. In Jesus' precious name. Amen.

17

Snares to the Christian

Matthew 7:13-14

"Enter ye in at the strait gate: for wide is the gate, and broad is the way, that leadeth to destruction, and many there be which go in thereat: Because strait is the gate, and narrow is the way, which leadeth unto life, and few there be that find it."

I am sure all of us realize and the way we tell we have gone from youth to the adult world is when we find out for the first time we are not indestructible. It is then we find out for the first time that our lives do in fact, hang by a slender thread. In the past several weeks, I have heard of more terrible deaths and diseases. I don't think I have ever heard of a time when there were so many people with cancer. On top of all that, there are all kinds of accidents taking people's lives. We finally learn when we get out of our young years, that all of that can happen to us. There are all kinds of peril in our roadway as we live our lives. As David said to Jonathan, surely there is but a step between me and death.

The other night as I was going home after studying at the church, something caused me to think what if I just turned my car and hit someone head on. My life was gone in a split second. There was my family to think about. The thought ran through me and caused a chill. I thought that could very easily happen. There was a time in my life when I thought that could have happened to someone else, but now I realize it can happen to me. Maybe the Lord was telling me to be careful. Maybe he was telling me to slow down danger was ahead. I don't know, but I thought it could happen to me. There are all kinds of peril in the life of a Christian between his profession of faith until he gets to heaven. There are a lot of things that are a danger to us in our Christian life and Christian experiences.

The devil is a roaring lion seeking whom he may devour. (I Peter 5:8) He is smart, intelligent, beautiful, pleasing and enticing enough to deceive the very elect. I think that is why the apostle said, take heed lest ye fall. I think the devil is working overtime today to keep as many people as he possible can from coming to know the Lord Jesus Christ as their personal Savior. He does not want you to be saved. He wants you to go on in the life you are now living deceiving you into thinking this is the life for you and finally snatch your soul into an eternity in hell. He does not want you to know Jesus Christ. If he can't keep you from knowing Christ and from learning about Jesus Christ, he will do all he possibly can to keep you from the adjustments in your life and meeting the conditions that are necessary for discipleship.

I don't know how you feel about how a person gets saved, but I wouldn't give you a nickel for this cheap, easy believism. It is not enough just to believe Jesus Christ was the Son of God. The devil believes that. In fact, he believes it so strongly that the scripture says, the devil believes and he trembles. Very few of us tremble at the thought of God. There are certain conditions that an individual has to make to become a disciple of the Lord Jesus Christ. So if he cannot keep you from learning about Jesus Christ he will keep you from meeting those conditions necessary to be a disciple. Have you ever watched a football game on television and a player took off running before he really had a hold of the ball? He was so eager to make a touchdown, he started running before he ever got the ball in his hands. Have you seen a hunter pull a trigger before he had aim on the game he was hunting? I had to give up hunting. I used to go quail hunting and there never was a covey of quail that didn't come up that didn't scare me to death. I have shot more holes in my dogs, trees, cars and trucks. They just scared me to death when they would fly up and I would watch them until they flew out of sight. I had already emptied the gun in the ground. People are so eager sometimes that they really don't take aim or know what they are doing. There are people who rush forward to make a decision or a public profession of the Lord Jesus Christ before they know him as personal Savior. There is a large organization in the world today that deals primarily in the evangelism of children. They meet in homes after school, meet with young people, and talk about the romance and beauty of winning small children to the Lord. They do it this way. They take three pieces of colored paper. The hold the black sheet and say this is your heart without Jesus Christ. They hold up the white piece of paper and say this is the heart of the Lord Jesus Christ and with the red paper they say this is the blood that Jesus shed to turn your heart from black to white, would you like to have a heart like Jesus? Of course, they all say yes and they are considered to be saved. Some people being eager to do things like that, cause people to enter into a relationship without ever really knowing the person they are supposed to have this relationship with.

So religion can very easily become a system of ritual and stressing rules and ceremonies. I want to share with you about 2 or 3 things that are snares to the Christian. First of all, the greatest peril to the lost person is to be indifferent. If you don't know Christ as your personal Savior, the most dangerous thing you can do is nothing. Jesus said in verse 14 of our text, "Enter ye at the strait gate". It takes effort to enter the gate. It takes effort to become a Christian. It takes effort to do what needs to be done to go to heaven. But all you have to do to go to hell is nothing. Men are naturally lost without God and have no hope. To get right with God requires effort. It requires action. Jesus said, "I am the way". That is true, but it takes action to enter the way. There is only one way to God and those who try some other way to God, the scripture says... is the same as a thief or robber". But broad is the way that leadeth to destruction. (Verse 13) It is a great danger to folks who think the world is thinking the way they think. For example, everyone in my age group is doing what I'm doing, so I'm safe in the crowd or I'm popular and it seems my whole world is living the way I am and the road is pretty smooth. It is no good to be walking on a smooth path if it is not leading to the destination you want to reach.

An older man stood in a church service to give his testimony. He wanted to receive Christ but something kept telling him he would have to give too much. He had a battle going trying to decide whether or not to become a Christian. Finally, he stood up and said I'm going to jerk away from the devil. What he said was exactly right, he had to take himself and jerk away from the devil. The devil had a hold of him and was constantly after him. That is exactly what it takes to become a Christian, it takes effort. To enter the strait gate takes effort but to enter the broad gate takes no effort at all.

The second danger is listening to false teachers. Matthew 7:15-20 "Beware of false prophets, which come to you in sheep's clothing, but inwardly they are ravening wolves. Ye shall know them by their fruits. Do men gather grapes of thorns or figs of thistles? Even so every good tree bringeth forth good fruit; but a corrupt tree bringeth forth evil fruit. A good tree cannot bring forth evil fruit; neither can a corrupt tree bring forth good fruit. Every tree that bringeth not forth good fruit is hewn down and cast into the fire. Wherefore their fruits ye shall know them." Jesus said, I am the way, but he also said, I am the truth. Now there is just as much danger of missing the truth as there is in missing the way. Jesus said beware of those who come as sheep but are in fact ravening wolves. There is a danger of missing the truth. The devil is a liar. He is the father of lies and he stands at every cross road and he is given out false directions. The spirit of Christ is in the business of leading people to God and giving the right directions. Jesus Christ alone is the truth. A man doesn't have to exercise a lot of effort to go the wrong way. I remember one day I was travelling to Knoxville and remember the road was in bad shape. As I drove, I noticed that the road had been fixed.

Come to find out I was on the wrong road all the time. When I went back to the starting point and got on the right road it was the same bumpy road I had traveled many times before. It doesn't take much effort to get on the wrong road. We are told to beware of false teachers and how to detect them. By their fruits ye shall know them. They can be morally upright, respectable citizens and leaders in the community and still be false teachers. Jesus said what kind of fruit are they bearing? What are they doing for the kingdom of God? He tells us to inspect their fruits and see if they are wolves or sheep.

Finally, another great peril to the Christian life is the danger of profession without practice. Let's pick up reading again in verse 21-24 "Not everyone that saith unto me, Lord, Lord, shall enter into the kingdom of heaven; but he that doeth the will of my Father which is in heaven. Many will say to me in that day, Lord, Lord, have we not prophesied in thy name? And in thy name have cast out devils? And in thy name done many wonderful works? And then will I profess unto them, I never knew you: depart from me, ye that work iniquity. Therefore whosoever heareth these sayings of mine, and doeth them, I will liken him unto a wise man, which built his house upon a rock:"It seems this particular warning was to Christians. He was saying don't profess something unless you are willing to practice it. Not everyone that says Lord, Lord will enter the kingdom of heaven. This reminds me of the Negro spiritual which says, Everyone's talking about heaven, ain't nobody going there. That is exactly what Jesus is saying right here. Everybody that talks about it is not going. My father use to tell the story and don't know if it was true, but he told it. There was a colored preacher preaching a funeral one time and he never like to say anything bad about a fellow. At the same time, he didn't have the disposition to preach a man into heaven if he didn't know if the man was a Christian. He was in a predicament. He began to preach the funeral and he said these words, "We are here today to eulogize Rufus Brown. I shore hope that he is going where I spec he ain't." And so Jesus said not everybody that says Lord, Lord identifies with the church and is going to heaven. Jesus said I am the way, the truth and the life. It is easy to preach but hard to live it. It is easy to talk about being a Christian and taking on all the responsibility of being a Christian. When it comes to living what we believe it is a different story. We may preach with power, perhaps talk about the truths of God. We believe in the fundamentals. Often when it comes to living, what we preach is a different story. Some say it is heresy to preach sinless perfection. That may be true, but it is also a heresy to preach a man can live as he wants to and go to heaven. The greatest illustration of that just hit me this week.

When Jesus gathered his disciples together, he said one of you is going to betray me. And if you pay attention to what they answered you will learn something that is a great warning to every Christian. He said one of you men is a traitor. One of you has been a devil from the very beginning and one of you is going to betray me. The disciples didn't jump up and say, I know who it is. They didn't say, I have been expecting Judas for a long time. I noticed how he had been drifting in his preaching. What did they say? They said, Lord, is it I?" They had absolutely no inclination that it was Judas and Judas was with them every day. He was preaching and testifying with them. He was a devil and they didn't know. That is a warning to every Christian.

I don't know what caused you to become a Christian, but I would like to tell you why I became a Christian. I heard a preacher one night talk about the sure foundation. I heard him talk about that foundation, no other man can build. There is no other foundation, except that foundation which is laid by Christ Jesus. For the first time, I knew, without a shadow of a doubt, that I was not on that sure foundation. He is the foundation and he furnished the materials for us to build our lives, but it is up to us to decide what kind of life we are going to build. When I consider the expensive foundation, can we build anything less than the best upon that foundation? Jesus is the firm foundation and all else is sinking sand. We must build soon. The sooner the build the better we are. We must select the building materials with care. We don't just build for fair weather because the storms of life are sure to come. Paul gives us a list of materials. He said there is gold, silver, precious stone, hay, wood and stubble. It is up to us which of those materials we want. A wise builder makes sure of his foundation. He listens to the architect. God's word is the blueprint. When the building is finished the architect is going to inspect it and pass his judgment on it. Jesus said the word that I have spoken the same shall judge you. Paul said one foundation. No man can lay any other foundation except that which is laid in Jesus Christ. Some build like the moralist. He has a good building, but a sorry foundation. Some are like the hypocrite who pretends that his life is built on a good foundation when in fact it is sinking sand. I thank God that there are a multitude of people who found the sure foundation and have built a life and built it well.

If you have not accepted Christ as your personal Savior, I invite you to build your life on the foundation of God.

Prayer: Our Heavenly Father, we thank you for this privilege of sharing together in this fellowship. We thank you for each one in this service. We pray we have profited from this time together. I thank you for the word and the Holy Spirit. I thank you there are still eager ears to hear thy word. I pray that you would speak to that heart which is warm and open to you. I pray that you would give that one who wants to come to you this opportunity to receive Christ as their personal Savior. In your blessed name I pray. Amen.

18

So Great A Salvation

Hebrews 2:1-6

"Therefore we ought to give the more earnest heed to the things which we have heard, lest at any time we should let them slip. For if the word spoken by angels was stedfast, and every transgression and disobedience received a just recompense of reward; How shall we escape, if we neglect so great salvation, which at the first began to be spoken by the Lord and was confirmed unto us by them that heard him; God also bearing them witness, both with signs and wonders, and with divers miracles, and gifts of the Holy Ghost, according to his own will? For unto the angels hath he not put in subjection the world to come, whereof we speak? But one in a certain place testified, saying, what is man, that thou art mindful of him? Or the son of man, that thou visitest him?"

The scripture says we can hear and hear again and never pay attention to those things we hear. Never give heed to the things we hear. And finally we let those things slip completely out of our mind. I believe there are a great number of people in the world today who are literally slipping into hell. Slipping because they are not willful and determined to go, but because they simply do not have the good logical sense applied to spiritual things that they do to physical things; and not giving heed to those things they let them slip. Letting them slip, the Bible says in verse 3," How shall we escape, if we neglect so great salvation...?"

I read an illustration of a great ocean liner and in the midst of her journey, a man fell overboard this great ship. Immediately all the life boats were beginning to drop into the sea. They began to drop ropes and lifesaving devices. Finally, they found the man, put the rope under his arms and through the pulley on the ship. They began to pull him out of the drowning condition and bring him to safety. Just as he got to the rail of the ship, the rope slipped and the man fell across the bow of the life boat and fell into the sea never to surface again. They never found him. I believe that is an illustration of many people today who have been brought to the very threshold of salvation. They have come to know and acknowledge the fact that they are sinners. All of us must bow to what the Bible says, for all have sinned and come short of the glory of God. John says if we say we have no sin we are liars and make God a liar. All of us are sinners. Men have come to the very threshold of acknowledging the fact they are sinners. Then they have admitted that the finished work of the Lord Jesus Christ would save them from that sinful condition. They have trembled with the conviction of the Holy Spirit of God and have steadfastly refused to make a decision for Jesus Christ. Having been brought to the very threshold of salvation, they slip into hell. They did not hate Christ. Those people who do not know him as Savior do not hate him. The people who do not go to church do not hate Jesus Christ, they merely neglect him. They merely neglect so great salvation. They do not disbelieve the Bible, it is just simply a matter of putting off getting right with God. They do not prefer to go to hell over heaven they just neglect saying yes to Jesus Christ. Not bitterly rejecting the Lord Jesus Christ but rather blindly neglecting him and finally slipped into hell drifting to eternal death, doom and damnation.

The words of our text in verse 3 which says, "...we ought to give more earnest heed to the things which we have heard, lest at any time we should let them slip", corresponds to the scripture found in Proverbs 29:1, "He that being often reproved hardenth his neck, shall suddenly be destroyed and that without remedy."

Perhaps it confirms the words of Jesus in Mark 8:36-37 "For what shall it profit a man, if he shall gain the whole world, and lose his own soul? Or what shall a man give in exchange for his soul?" The truth of the matter is that more folks will go to hell than to heaven. How can a preacher make a statement like that? Jesus said so in Matthew 7:13-14 "Enter ye in at the strait gate: for wide is the gate, and broad is the way, that leadeth to destruction, and many there be which go in thereat: Because strait is the gate, and narrow is the way, which leadeth unto life, and few there be that find it." Jesus said wide is the road travelled to hell and many are on it and narrow is the path to heaven and few travel upon it. So more people go to hell than go to heaven. Why? Because of neglect. They do not set out to do that. It is because they neglect to do things that need to be done in order to assure them that they will go to heaven. Just like folks neglect their health, their home, their husband, their wife and children until they lose one or the other. The same is true about their spiritual life. The writer of Hebrews said, "...give the more earnest heed..." In other words, pay attention to those things which you have heard. I trust you will give earnest heed as I call your attention to a few points. First, the salvation which God provides is great. It is referred to as so great salvation in our text. Why is it so great? First of all, the origin of salvation makes it a great and wonderful salvation because of the creator. Folks live as though salvation was some kind of scheme that was designed in the halls of Congress. Brother, this salvation, which you and I know, was not conceived in Congress. It was not something that was debated on the floor of a conference or convention. It was not something that was thought up in the rooms of Parliament. The very glorious circle throne of heaven was the origin of salvation. It is great because of where it came from. It came from the palace of the immutable, eternal, ever glorifying God. Salvation did not come out of necessity, but it came because of the love of the holy God, the undying love of a powerful God for our poor, lost, hell bound soul. God so loved us that he gave his only begotten son so that we would not perish. It was not something that man devised in his mythology to make excuses and room for the failures of man. It came from God and the love of God. No greater love hath no man that a man will lay down his life for his friends. This is the love of God, not that we love him, but that he loved us. While we were yet sinners, Christ died for us. When we were far off from God he loved us. That makes salvation great.

Salvation is great because of what it cost. Salvation is a costly thing. When you hear a preacher talk about salvation being free, it is, it is free as the air you breathe to you, but it cost something. Whether a man is pardoned or unpardoned it costs. If man is forgiven of his sin, the cost of his sin has fallen upon the sacrifice of God which was his Son the Lord Jesus Christ. He took it and he who knew no sin became sin for us. If you have been pardoned and are a child of God then it cost Jesus Christ his very own life. God's only begotten Son paid the price. If you have not been pardoned, and are not a child of God, all of that sin will rest upon your head and will cost you an eternity in hell. Salvation was great in its cost. I am glad I realized I could not pay for my sin. I am glad I realized there was nothing I could do that would merit me one moment in heaven. I realized in me, as Paul said, there dwell no good thing. When I realized I was lost and in the lost condition I would go to hell, and when I realized I could not save myself then brother, I didn't come to town on a load of watermelons. I have got sense enough to go to the one who could save me and that one is Jesus Christ. I will go to heaven not because of anything I did or deserve but because I was willing to bow at the feet of Jesus and say God be merciful to me a sinner. That's free. Oh the price, that it cost to bring me that free salvation. Paul said, we are not bought with corruptible things such as silver or gold, but we were bought with the precious blood of the Lamb without spot or blemish, the Lord Jesus Christ. God's Son paid the price and it was costly. When he died, the sun refused to shine and the very world quaked in terror.

God's salvation is great because it is complete. Colossians 2:9-10 "For in him dwelleth all the fullness of the Godhead bodily. And ye are complete in him, which is the head of all principality and power:" Complete means all that I need. All I need for my forgiveness of sin is in Jesus Christ. Forgiveness of sin – the indwelling of the Holy Spirit of God; joy, peace, assurance, the privilege of prayer, sanctification, power and victory over sin. All of this and heaven too. It is complete, it is great.

What about the neglect? How shall we escape if we neglect, the Bible says, so great salvation? Isn't it rather strange the procrastination of sinners: putting off, putting off, and putting off? I believe the very angels in heaven must absolutely live in amazement when they view sinners sinking into hell, putting off through their neglect. If we could just think in spiritual terms as we do in physical terms we would all get saved. If you knew the road you were traveling down in your automobile going home from church would drop you into a sink hole and you could never get out, you would turn around and go some other way. If you knew that if you went to work tomorrow on your particular job you were going to fall and your life be taken from you, you simply would not go. Yet folks live, knowing that the Bible is true and what God said is true and keep right on going. Neglecting, neglecting, neglecting saying I'll make a death bed confession. Don't trust a death bed confession. It is a last resort and God can save you at anytime, anywhere. I don't put much stock in death bed confessions. I think they come out of fear and not out of the love for God. I would be willing to say that if a man made a death bed confession and all of the sudden he got better, God would be the last thing he would think about. I have seen it happen. But because he thought he was going to die he called on God just like you would climb out of a fire escape if your house was on fire. People use the Lord Jesus Christ as a fire escape out of hell. They just simply neglect and put it off.

God's love is rich. God's love is wonderful and he offers us every opportunity to be saved. Every opportunity you have to get saved and you don't take it, that opportunity is lost to you forever. Now another opportunity may or may not come, but that opportunity will never be yours again. Until the time will come when there will be no more opportunities to be saved. Like our own common sense tells us and the writer of II Samuel said, it is like water spilt on the ground it cannot be gathered up again. How many opportunities have you trodden underfoot? The Bible says behold now is the accepted time and today is the day of salvation. You ever notice God deals with now, he never says tomorrow. God never said, I want you to be saved tomorrow. God never promised you that you could be saved tomorrow. God always says now. Now is the time of salvation. Today is the day of salvation. Every tick of the clock is God's opportunity to be saved and every tick of the clock refused is a lost opportunity to become a part of the kingdom of God.

Felix, the governor, faced an opportunity from God. He heard the Apostle Paul proclaim a very simple message of God's love for the sinner. The Holy Spirit so stirred that governor's heart, that Felix trembled under the conviction of the Holy Spirit of God, but he trampled underfoot the love of God. As far as we know, he never had another opportunity to be saved. King Agrippa, the man who heard a sermon from the lips of the Apostle Paul was stirred in his heart. He even came to a place where he said almost thou persuadest me to be a Christian and he was never persuaded, as far as we know, and his opportunity never came back.

Neglect means that there is no escape from a hardened heart. Delay or putting it off is a disease. Hebrews 3:12-13 says "Take heed, brethren, lest there be any of you an evil heart of unbelief, in departing from the living God. But exhort one another daily, while it is called today; lest any of you be hardened through the deceitfulness of sin." He is simply saying that when you hear the gospel of the Lord Jesus Christ and do not turn to it your heart becomes hardened that much more. No one can escape having a cold, stony, hardened heart. Delay gives sin the opportunity to harden man's heart. You say, brother, I am as tenderhearted today as I was 20 years ago. That is not true. No man remains unconverted and tenderhearted. You cannot do it. If you remain unconverted you will have a hard heart; just like clay turns to iron and water turns to ice and putty turns to rock. The gospel of God is depicted as a two-edged sword which cuts both ways. Every time we hear it man's heart is either turned to God or turned away. You can say, preacher, I came to church, heard you preach, got up and left just exactly like I came. No you didn't. If you left, you walked out just a little bit closer to sinning away your day of grace. You walked out just a little bit closer to that time God will say that's it. That's it, never again will I stir your heart and save you. You do not walk out unchanged. No sermon ever preached left men unchanged – either hearts were tender or their hearts were hardened.

In closing let me share these verses of scripture found in Hebrews 10:26-31" For if we sin willfully after that we have received the knowledge of the truth, there remaineth no more sacrifice for sins, but a certain fearful looking for of judgment and fiery indignation, which shall devour the adversaries. He that despised Moses' law died without mercy under two or three witnesses: of how much sorer punishment, suppose ye, shall he be thought worthy, who hath trodden underfoot the Son of God, and hath counted the blood of the covenant, wherewith he was sanctified, an unholy thing, and hath done despite unto the Spirit of grace? For we know him that hath said, Vengeance belongeth unto me, I will recompense, said the Lord. And again, The Lord shall judge his people. It is a fearful thing to fall into the hands of the living God." Hebrews 2 said give earnest heed to the things which you have heard lest you let them slip. He says later in verse 26 of Hebrews 10 that God has done all he can do. Jesus died once for sin. He will never be crucified again. Do you hear the truth? If you reject him all you have is a fearful looking for the judgment. If a man rejected the Law of Moses and put to death by two or three witnesses, he asked you to use your mind for a minute and just suppose how much more worthy is a man of punishment if he trample underfoot the Son of God.

How shall a man escape if he neglect so great salvation? He can't escape. The scripture says, today if you will hear his voice, harden not your heart. It is saying if you hear and you do not respond, you are hardening your heart. Be not deceived, God is not mocked for whatsoever a man soweth that shall he also reap. Several years ago in a small town in Pennsylvania the great dam was about to break and the people were warned time and time again. It didn't break. On this one occasion they were being warned that the dam could break at any moment and you know what most people said? The reason so many people died that day, when the dam gave loose they said, you can't scare us. Today if you hear his voice, harden not your heart. Don't adopt the philosophy of a fool which says, Preacher, you can't scare me. That's right, I can't. All of you who hear the sound of my voice know for a fact that the Bible is true. What God said is true. You know that the wages of sin is death. You know that a soul that sinneth, it shall die. You also know the only way to be saved is to receive Christ as your personal Savior. You know Christ is your only hope. I am not trying to scare you but to invite you to use your logical good sense and fall at the feet of the Lord Jesus Christ and in faith, before it is too late, get right with God. Seek ye the Lord while he may be found. Call upon the Lord while he is near. Let the wicked forsake his way and the unrighteousness man his thoughts and God will abundantly pardon. Give the more earnest heed to things which you have heard, lest at any time you should let them slip. Don't let this opportunity slip away from you. If you do not know Christ as your personal Savior, give earnest heed to that which ye have heard. Call upon the Lord while He is near and he will abundantly pardon.

Prayer: Our Heavenly Father, we thank you today for the Lord Jesus Christ who became our sacrifice for sin. We thank you Father that you knowing we could not pay our own penalty for sin, provided the lamb without spot or blemish; who satisfied God's justice and turned away the wrath of sin. Father, we thank you today it is so simple and that all we have to do is to receive, by faith, that which you did for us. I pray today, if there is one who does not know you as his or her personal Savior that today would be the time they would be the time they would simply give heed to the things they have heard. All of us Father have heard the message of salvation time and time again. Father, we pray that you will help us not to turn away, but to give heed to things we have heard, lest we let them slip. For how shall we escape if we neglect so great salvation? Reach out and touch that heart that needs to be brought into thy love and needs to become a part of the family of God and salvation from sin. Claim that soul for your very own. Help us to yield ourselves to thee. If there is sin in our lives, help is to confess it. Help us to walk straight. Use these words to bring honor and glory to your name and salvation to souls. We ask all of this in Christ's name. Amen.

19

Behold the Lamb of God

John 1:29-37

We have in John 1:29-37 John the Baptist's introduction of Jesus. "The next day John seeth Jesus coming unto him, and said, behold the Lamb of God, which taketh away the sin of the world. This is he of whom I said, after me cometh a man which is preferred before me: for he was before me. And I knew him not: but that he should be made manifest to Israel, therefore am I come baptizing with water. And John bare record, saying, I saw the Spirit descending from heaven like a dove, and it abode upon him. And I knew him not: but he that sent me to baptize with water, the same aid unto me, Upon whom thou shalt see the Spirit descending, and remaining on him, the same is he which baptizeth with the Holy Ghost. And I saw, and bare record that this is the Son of God. Again the next day after John stood, and two of his disciples; And looking upon Jesus as he walked, he saith, Behold the Lamb of God! And the two disciples heard him speak, and they followed Jesus."

Some people say that John the Baptist was born to say one sentence; that he was born to make one exclamation. The ministry of John the Baptist was like Peter's ministry. He rose suddenly in the barren desert, he delivered his message and just as quickly he disappeared off the scene. His ministry was very quick and sudden and it seemed he was born for one purpose. God chose John the Baptist as the one who would introduce his Son the Lord Jesus Christ to the world. With the introduction by

John the Baptist, Jesus began his public ministry. Had you been chosen of God to introduce the Lord Jesus Christ how would you have introduced him? Had God said to you I want you to go out and when you see the Lord coming, I want you to introduce the Lord Jesus Christ to the world in words they will not forget, what would you say?

I am sure some people would say, Behold the man who can feed the poor. Behold a man who can feed all of those who are hungry. What a hay day the reporters would have with a front page caption like that. Behold a man that can take loaves and fishes and can feed the poor. I have come to believe that our government has a complex about those who do not work or those who do not care; those who will not support themselves through honest work. I think it is a wonderful thing for all of those in the world, through sickness or some other thing out of their control to be supported and helped. We have a guilt complex in America, I think that sends the rest of us to work for those who will not. We have seen in the past few years tens of thousands different welfare programs that absolutely grow more insane as they are being implemented by our local governments. Had we had the opportunity to introduce a man who could feed the poor what a great enthusiastic way we could have introduced our Lord.

Perhaps we could introduce him like this, Behold the man that can call down legions of angels. Jesus said on one occasion, I have but to say the word and I can call down 72,000 angels to do my bidding. Can you imagine what devastation 72,000 could have caused at the word of God? So perhaps we could have introduced the Lord as a man with power to call down legions of angels from heaven. We could have said, behold a man who can heal the sick. Certainly any man who has a reputation of being able to heal the sick would have a great multitude of followers. Behold the man who can open the eyes of the blind, ears of the deaf and can cause those who are crippled to walk again. Behold a man that can control nature. Behold a man who can go out to the sea when it is raging and say, peace be still and the waves suddenly obey his voice and the sea becomes calm. Can you imagine how exciting it would be to introduce the Lord in so many ways? A man that can feed the poor, heal the sick, call legions of angels and a man who has the power over nature.

John the Baptist was chosen of God to introduce his Son. John the Baptist said these words, "Behold the Lamb of God which taketh away the sin of the world." Let's think for a moment about the sin of the world. Here is a man from God, John, who said, Jesus was the Lamb of God and came for one purpose to take away the sin of the world. God says that is what is wrong with the world. God says it's not inflation, it's not suffering and diseases, it's not crime or corruption in high places, but sin is what is wrong with the world. What is at the root of all crime, inflation, violence, bloodshed, and sickness – sin? I am amazed at how for so many years ministers who preach the gospel or supposed to preach the gospel have totally ignored or buried and forgotten the old doctrines that our forefathers preached. Now that the world is in such terrible shape with crime rate, inflation rate and with all the other things happening in the world, more and more ministers are becoming aware again of that old doctrine our forefathers preached and that today's psychologist laugh at. Ministers are becoming aware that sin is exactly what is wrong with the world today. The things that our forefathers preached: total depravity, sin nature, that's what they preached and that is what God said was wrong with us and people are becoming aware of the monster we are facing in the world is exactly what is described in the Bible. Sin. Out preachers in the past called it total depravity. They preached that people are born sinners. They are not just entering in some kind of sin as they live, but sin has entered our whole personality and emotion. Man is totally depraved. They preached sin, heaven and hell. Do you know when hell became so great in our streets? When the hell left our pulpits, it went into the streets. If there was hell preached from the pulpit you didn't find it in the homes and in the streets. Now that it is not in the pulpit, we find our homes and streets filled with it. Those who hold on to the fundamental truths of the word of God still preach it. Our problem is exactly what the Bible says – Sin.

I read something the other day from the Minnesota crime commission report. I want to read you what the crime report said, "What we call delinquency or delinquent behavior is not anything new. What we call delinquent behavior is as old as man itself. It is not something that just moronic segment of our society is liable for but no infant is born a finished product. Every baby starts life a savage. Every child is born with urges, aggressiveness, anger, fear, love, no control, completely self-centered and he wants what he wants when he wants it. He wants his bottle, he wants his mother's attention, he wants his uncle's watch and if you deny them that they see with rage and aggression and would commit murder were they not helpless." It goes on to say, "The child is dirty, has no morals, no knowledge, no skill, they are all born delinquents and if permitted to continue to grow up like that, every one of them will be criminals, thieves, killers and rapists. Every child as he grows up it is normal for him to fight, grab, tear things apart, and talk back, to disobey. Every child must grow out of delinquent behavior." The report finished by saying these words, "what we need then is discipline". Discipline in the homes, discipline in the school because every child is a delinquent and must grow out of delinquency. What are they saying? They are saying what the Bible says, men are born sinners. Men are born totally depraved. Unless something happens to that individual they will become increasing more evil as they get older. Therefore, they conclude what we need is discipline. And John the Baptist came to say, Behold the Lamb of God, which came to take away the sin of the world.

I am reminded of what Paul said in Romans 14:14, "I know and am persuaded by the Lord Jesus, that there is nothing unclean of itself..." I got to thinking about that. You mean to tell me that whiskey is alright; that gambling is alright; that adultery is alright?

Then I read it again. Paul said, I am persuaded that nothing within itself is unclean. So I began to say how I can make that all work out in my thinking. So let's take alcohol for example. There is nothing wrong with alcohol. There could be no practice of medicine without it. It is the solvent that carries almost all of our medicines. There is nothing wrong with alcohol until you add sin to it. You add sin to it and you have a disaster. Playing cards, dominoes and checkers is not wrong until you add sin to it. The gun was one of the finest instruments invented until you add sin to it. You add sin to the gun and you have murder, bloodshed, blackmail and all the other things. To take sin out of those things; to take sin out of our heart, God's remedy for man is to Behold the Lamb of God.

How does it work? God took away our penalty, our judgment when he took upon himself our sin. More than that, he took upon himself the very wrath of God for our sins. He bore out iniquities on the tree. It is in our accepting that grace and accepting what Jesus Christ did for us that the stain of sin is washed away. Our souls are cleansed and he forgives us our iniquity. He creates in us a new heart and a new life; not only in this life but in the life to come. Did you ever think about the fact that when Jesus went to heaven he didn't go alone? When Jesus went to heaven he put his arm around the thief he saved on the cross. The man who, died beside the Lamb of God, went to heaven with Jesus. He died beside the Lamb of God who takes away the sin of the world. Tremendous thought.

John the Baptist had the rare privilege of pointing to the whole world and saying, that's the Lamb of God; that's the Son of God. There is not a greater privilege in the whole world than to point to the Lamb of God. That to me is my greatest joy that through the word of God, I point you and others to the Lamb of God and say to you, Behold the Lamb of God which takes away the sin of the world. That was what John the Baptist was called to do. Will you trust him? Will you receive him? Will you accept him as your personal Savior? Behold the Lamb of God today.

Prayer: Heavenly Father, we thank you for every blessing of life. We thank you for the Lamb of God which takes away the sin of the world. We thank you, father, that one day we met the Lamb of God and that his blood was applied to our hearts and our lives and our sins were washed away. We thank you that we can know the time the day and the hour that we can know by our personal experience that our sins are washed away. We thank you for the Lamb that he was without spot or blemish. We thank you that he was able to satisfy the justice of God. We thank you that the Lamb was willing to become obedient even unto death. We thank you that Lamb, precious in the sight of God, was willing to bear our transgressions. He was willing to be wounded and bruised for our iniquities. We thank you for the privilege of pointing others to God. We thank you that Christ comes and does in fact say, behold I stand at the door and knock. If any man will open the door, I will come in and sup with him and he with me. Father, we thank you for the Lamb of God.

20

Do You Care?

Psalms 142:1-7

"I cried unto the Lord with my voice; with my voice unto the Lord did I make my supplication. I poured out my complaint before him; I shewed before him my trouble. When my spirit was overwhelmed within me, then thou knewest my path. In the way wherein I walked have they privily laid a snare for me. I looked on my right hand, and beheld, but there was no man that would know me: refuge failed me; no man cared for my soul. I cried unto thee, O Lord: I said, Thou art my refuge and my portion in the land of the living. Attend unto my cry; for I am brought very low: deliver me from my persecutors; for they are stronger than I Bring my soul out of prison, that I may praise thy name: the righteous shall compass me about; for thou shalt deal bountifully with me."

I would like to share with you an experience out of David's life; one of deliverance. One of my favorite characters in the Old Testament is David. The reason is David is so human. He is very much like we are. David was certainly no perfect saint. David was a man who would be a great sinner one time and a saint the next. He was the man who could write the 23rd Psalm, the Lord is my shepherd I shall not want. And then he could cry out, no man cares for my soul in verse 4 of our text. It was a little bit like the New Testament character Peter, who was sort of one day all out and the next day maybe dragging his feet. In despair, in the

Psalm, David cries out. David is on the mountain top in one Psalm and laying in the valley in another.

There is one thing about David; he was always reaching out to God. Even in his sinful experiences, he cried out to God. He was always trying to be a better man. He was always trying to get a hold of the hand of God. It is sort of like the song, we hear, "I'm sometimes up and sometimes down, but praise God I'm heaven bound." That is the way many of us are: many times on the mountaintop, many times in the valley. But we are reaching up to God trying to see God in all our ways. I believe all of us are like David from time to time. All of us, at some point or another, give up on our soul. Have you ever come to a place where you said, there is nobody who cares about me? There is no one who cares if I go to heaven or hell. You have felt no one cares whether you are happy or not. People just don't really care about my soul.
I can remember an experience like that and if I didn't think it would embarrass my wife and children, I'd tell you about it. I remember a time when I didn't think anyone cared about my soul. I want to show you how wrong you are, if you have ever said as David said, no one cares for my soul.

First of all, let's go back to the very beginning. I want to say to you God cares about your soul. God cares about you as an individual. I went over to Cumberland Heights not too long ago to visit a man who was there trying to get help for his alcoholism. He didn't have the view of God that you and I have. He knew that God was mighty. He knew God made the heavens and the earth, but he could not bring himself to believe that with all the problems God has, certainly God couldn't care about him. He said don't tell me that the God who keeps this world going has the time to worry about me. He couldn't see God caring about a man with an addiction He could not grasp the idea that God cares about an individual soul. Back in the Garden of Eden, our parents Adam and Eve, sinned and fell from that place of perfectness and holiness with God. When they fell into sin, the disease of sin entered into the vein of the human race. Since the day of Adam's fall, all men are born sinners. Now God is a God of justice. God's law was broken. God's law had been violated. If he is a God of justice, then punishment must flow for the broken law. He would not be just by turning the other way. He had to punish that broken law. The punishment is God's eternal prison house that was prepared for Satan and his angels. A place called hell. But God looked down and saw men on their way to hell and in his compassion he said, I must do something about this. I must provide a way of escape. Therefore, I must find someone who can bear the sin of the human race. No it must be someone who has no sin, must be someone without sin and must be someone without spot or blemish. He looked over heaven and saw some prophets and they said send me. God knew they could not go because they were sinners. All of the men in the Old Testament were sinners. Who could go? God's eyes lighted upon his own begotten Son. God said, Son will you go? You are the only one without sin. You are the only sacrifice that could carry the sin of mankind. Jesus said, I'll go, I will leave heaven to go to earth and I'll die for man's sin. Don't you know that all of heaven cried out, No! Don't you know that Jesus Christ who was the only sinless creature of heaven; the one figure who all the angels did his bidding and the very glory of heaven shone around him, surely the angels said, No not you Lord. How could he send his Son to die for me? But God so loved the world that whosoever believeth in him should not perish but have everlasting life. John 3:16. Jesus came to earth and lived as a man. He became a man of sorrows acquainted with grief. He was mistreated, rejected and finally crucified on Calvary's cross and God saw it all.

Did you ever think about that? Did you ever think about God looking at his Son dying? Back during the war, many parents who received a telegram that said, 'we regret to inform you that your son has been killed in action'. What a hard blow that was to those who received that kind of news. But they didn't see their son die. They didn't see the machine gun that tore out his heart. They didn't see the blood. They just read a telegram. But God saw the blood. God saw the cruel beatings. God saw the hands as they were tore open by nails. God saw his brow being broken. God saw the hole in his side made by the spear. God saw it all, looked at it and said, I care for your soul. God was saying on the cross I care for you. He was in Christ reconciling the world unto himself. Why else would he send his Son to die, except he loved you and me? God says today, look at Calvary. I gave my Son to save you from hell. Don't ever say no one cares for your soul, because God cares.

Secondly, the Lord Jesus Christ cares about your soul. Jesus was the highest figure in the heaven. He came from all the glory that was his and sped down to earth and became the humblest of men willing to be born of a virgin as a tiny babe. Did you ever think about the Holy Spirit taking the Son of God and reducing the Son of God to a tiny cell? Did you ever think of the condescension of God's Son? To be willing to leave heaven's door to be reduced to a tiny cell. Jesus was saying I love you and your soul. Jesus was laid in a manger as a tiny baby boy. If I could walk up to the manager, perhaps I would say, is this the one who created the heavens and the earth? Jesus said without me nothing was created that was created. Is he the one that created all of heaven? Yes, that tiny baby created the heavens and the earth. Is this the baby that rules the destiny of nations? Yes, it is God's only begotten Son. During his ministry, Jesus was called by every name. He was humiliated, rejected and betrayed. He was arrested and came before Pilate. The scripture says they made a crown of thorns and mockingly said if you are a king you must have a crown. They wove thorns into a crown and pushed it down upon his brow and the thorns tore into the flesh. They slapped him, spit upon him, beat him and finally laid the cruel cross on his shoulders that he might bear it to a place called Calvary. As he bore that cross and fell beneath the load. If you had been standing by the road and said, Lord why do you do all of this, he would have said because I love you. Because I love you.

A young boy had met the girl of his dreams and they were to be married. It was back in the day of horse and buggy. One day they went into town to get the marriage license. He loved that woman with all his heart. She loved him, a hard working country boy. While she was sitting in the wagon while he was taking care of business, something startled the horses and they began to run. The boy saw this team of horses coming down Main Street running wildly and he knew that his bride would be killed and he ran into the roadway in front of his horses and grabbed the bridle and hung on for dear life. The horses drug him, stepped on him and mutilated his body and he fell into the street. The woman jumped off the wagon, ran to him and as she bent down over him, his last words were, I loved you, didn't I. He was willing to give his life for his bride. Scripture says, Husbands love your wives as Christ loved the church and gave himself for it. That young boy was willing to give his life for his bride. Jesus loves us and cares about our souls.

Thirdly, the Holy Spirit cares about our soul. Not many people know much about the Holy Spirit. Let me say to you that the Holy Spirit is the third person of the Godhead. He is co-equal with God. The Holy Spirit of God works today in the hearts of God's people. He convicts those who are unsaved and guides those who are saved. Jesus said when I am gone, I will send the comforter to you and when he is come I will convict the world of righteousness and sin and of judgment to come. The Holy Spirit comes to you and he says, you're not right with God are you? You have sinned haven't you? Someday, you must face the judgment. In the pointing out of sin, he points us to the way of salvation and says you need a Savior. You need someone who can save you from that sin and the only one that can save you is at the right hand of God the Father. Accept him and be saved. The Holy Spirit speaks to every man. He has spoken to your heart many times. Some of you have responded to the Holy Spirit and some of you have rejected him. But all of us have heard him speak and he shows you the Savior.

Fourthly, the church cares for your soul. The church of Jesus Christ is a place of worship. It is a place where the saints of God gather and worship. It is more than that. The world is dying without hope outside of the Lord Jesus Christ. Church members are those who found the one who saves from sin. It is their business to tell others who are in need of a Savior who that Savior is. It is your responsibility, as a member of the body of Christ, to tell everyone who needs to hear the message that Jesus saves. In the book of Revelation, the scripture says, the spirit and the bride say come. Revelation 22:17. Who is the bride? The bride is the church of Jesus Christ. The church says come. The church wants to see you saved and that is why we are here.

Fifthly, people in heaven, care about your soul. The scripture says there is more rejoicing in heaven over one sinner that repenteth than ninety-nine who need no repentance. Luke 15:7. Why do they rejoice? Why does heaven rejoice when someone repents of their sin? Because they know what it is like. They are enjoying the wonderful things of heaven and they rejoice that you too will share it. They want you to join them. I don't know if people in heaven see everything that happens on earth. I wish I knew. I have a suspicion that they know when someone gets saved. A mother has a baby and sees that baby grow into a fine young boy. It is her hope and prayer that boy one day would walk the aisle of the church and receive Christ as his personal Savior. She prays and lives for that; to see a day when her children are safe in the arms of Jesus. She dies never having realized that dream. Sometime later that young boy, under the conviction of the Holy Spirit, walks the aisle of the church and receives Christ as his personal Savior. I believe the guardian angel of that boy goes to one of the mansions in heaven and says to that mother, your son just got saved this morning. I can hear that mother rejoicing all over heaven and tells those around her to come rejoice with me because my son just got saved. That mother will say one day he will be here rejoicing with me. Someday, I'll be reunited with my son again and we will have full fellowship and companionship.

Finally, people, in hell, care about your soul. That is a solemn thought. Jesus said there were two men, one a rich man and one a poor man. The rich man wore beautiful clothing and the poor man was not only poor but full of sores and he laid everyday at the rich man's gate and dogs came and licked his sores. He just begged for the crumbs that fell from the rich man's table. The scripture says in Luke 16:19 that the rich man died and went to hell. He didn't go to hell because he was rich and the poor man didn't go to heaven because he was poor. It had nothing to do with that. The rich man went to hell because he rejected Christ as his personal Savior. But in hell he lifted up his eyes in torment and looked across the great gulf that is fixed and he saw Lazarus in the bosom of Abraham and he said, "Father Abraham, send Lazarus that he may dip the tip of his finger in water and cool my tongue for I am tormented in this flame. Luke 16:24. Abraham told the rich man he cannot come to you for there is a great gulf fixed; you can't come here and neither can he come to you. The rich man said send him back to earth to my father's house and tell my brothers who have not received Christ as Savior, to accept Christ that they might not come to this place of burning. I don't want them to come. He said persuade them, beg them, do whatever you have to do but make sure my brothers do not come to this place of torment. Abraham said your brothers have had the same opportunity to hear the gospel as you did and they rejected it just like you did. They wouldn't listen to Moses and the prophets and they wouldn't listen to him even though he be raised from the dead. People in hell care about your soul. They don't want you to join them there. They know what an awful place it is.

There are a lot of people that care about your soul. God cares, Jesus Christ cares, the Holy Spirit cares, and the church cares, the people in heaven care and the people in hell care about your soul. The question is, do you care? Do you care about your own soul? How much is it worth? What profiteth a man, if he gained the whole world and loses his soul? God said the soul is worth more than the wealth of the whole world. We can't even imagine that kind of wealth. What if you had it all? All the wealth that existed would not be of the same value as your soul. Do you care whether or not you go to heaven? You say, yeah, I'm going to be saved. How do you know if you put it off till some convenient time, how do you know the Holy Spirit will draw you to salvation? My spirit will not always strive with man Genesis 6:3. How do you know you will live tomorrow? How do you know you will be alive tonight? I was thinking this week of the people in this community that have died in automobile accidents in the past five years. I thought of those people like my neighbors, who were one minute driving and enjoying the countryside and then the next gone. In a split second both were gone to eternity. You may not really care if you go to heaven or hell. But if you care, you'll never find a more perfect time then today to accept Christ as your personal Savior and insure you eternal residence.

If you hear my voice, harden not your heart. No one ever cared for you like Jesus. No one ever cared for me like Jesus; There's no other friend so kind as He. No one else could take the sin and darkness from me; O how much He cared for me. (Lyrics and Composer: Charles Frederick Weigle, 1932)

Prayer: Our Heavenly Father, we praise you today that you've done so much that we might hear the gospel, that we might be prepared to live eternity in a saved condition. No one ever cared for us Father, like you did. You gave us the church, the Holy Spirit, friends and you gave us all the things to point to the way of salvation. Father, I realize today that you care about our soul. If we look at the cross, we see just how much you care. We know that the Holy Spirit cares because he is acting today to speak to our hearts. Father, help the church to care. I pray you will help those that do not know Christ as their personal Savior to care. Help them to consider the value of their soul. Help them, Father, to reach out to the Lord Jesus Christ and make them safe and sure for now and to eternity. We'll praise you for all that you have done and what you are doing to do, in the name of Jesus Christ our Savior, we pray. Amen.

21

Sin of a Christian

Matthew 1:21

I was to preach on sin today. I suppose that is a good topic for a preacher to preach. But I am not going to preach on the sin of the world. It seems like when I try to preach about the things that are wrong in the world, I feel a little bit helpless because I don't think I'm changing anything. Today I am preaching on sin and in particularly to Christians who sin. The scripture says, "And she shall bring forth a son, and thou shalt call his name JESUS: for he shall save his people from their sins."

There are two kinds of sinners in this world. First, there is the lost sinner. The sinner who has never trusted the Lord Jesus Christ, who has never been born again, who has just simply left Jesus Christ out of their life. I hope none of you get carried away with a lot of the modern preaching that you hear. I've been hearing a lot of preaching lately that goes something like this: they say God is with us every hour of our lives that he is with us in every circumstance of our life and he goes with us to the sunset of life through death and then he carries us home to be with him in heaven. That is a beautiful statement, but they preach that as if it applied to everyone. Regardless of your position and regardless of your accepting or rejecting of Jesus Christ they apply that statement to everyone. I want to remind all of us that God has some wonderful promises in his word. He promised to be with us every step of our life, go with us through every crisis, go with us through death and carry us home to heaven, but those promises were made only to those who are born again believers. Those promises were not made to everybody. The modern preacher never mentions repentance toward God and faith in Jesus Christ. God does not and never will promise to go with an evil wicked man. It is simply not in the word of God. His promises are to the righteous and we need to lay aside any kind of thinking that would help us to believe that God loves everybody regardless of their life. God loves the sinner, God loves the lost, but his promises of salvation and his promises of blessing are to those who receive his Son as their personal Savior and to no one else. There are some lost sinners.

Then there are some saved sinners. When we come to the Lord Jesus Christ through repentance and faith, he saves us. He saves us from sin, he writes our names in the Lamb's Book of Life and we are safe as long as we are in the Lord Jesus Christ. God's promises are real and wonderful. He saves us from sin and gives us a new nature when we are saved. One of the things Christians don't understand when they are first saved is when God saves us and puts his nature within us the old nature doesn't run off and hide; the new nature doesn't kill the old nature. God doesn't do some kind of magic on us and our old feelings go away. They are with us until we die. A lot of times when a person gets saved, he feels like he ought to be saved from temptation, he ought to not ever want to do the things he did before and he finds that the old nature is there. He is still tempted, he is still weak in all points and when he yields to that he says I must not be saved. Christians need to understand that when they get saved, they still have that old nature. The Apostle Paul was God's greatest man and was afflicted with that old nature until he died. The Apostle Paul, and you know how wonderful he was and how many wonderful things he did for God, said on one occasion: the things I know I ought to do I don't do them and the things I know I ought not to do those are the things that I do. He is talking about the old nature. Sometimes the old nature gets the upper hand on us and when it does we sin.

Out text says, "...he shall save his people from their sins." Jesus came to save us from the root of sin. We are forgiven of those sins when we receive Christ as our personal Savior. There are some fruit of sin that we exhibit every day of our lives and they are forgiven by daily confessing our sin unto the Lord Jesus Christ. Lots of people think the saints of God are perfect; that the church members are perfect. Some people think they are better than anyone else if they are a member of a church. There are a lot of misconceptions about the word of God. There are some sins that you and I commit that we ought to lay at the feet of Jesus Christ. There are some sins of the saints. There are sins that we commit when we allow the old nature to get the upper hand. I want to talk about some of those today. I am not talking about the unsaved. I'm not talking about the man who doesn't go to church. I'm talking about you and me, members of the church. What are some of the sins of the saints?

The first one I want to talk about is worldliness. You have heard the word all of your life. Free Will Baptists use the word often in describing one's commitment to Jesus Christ and being delivered from worldliness. What does worldliness mean? Worldliness is anything in your personal life that comes between you and your commitment to the Lord Jesus Christ and to his church. A lot of things that Christians are involved in are not, in themselves, bad but they cause them to lose their commitment to Jesus Christ. I know a couple who went to church every time the doors were open. They both taught Sunday school and she worked in the Ladies Auxiliary. They were active in the church and could always be counted on by the church and by the Lord. After a few years, the woman was invited to join a civic organization. There is nothing wrong with a civic organization such as the Civitan, Kiwanis, Lions Club, etc. They are all good organizations, as far as I know. But it wasn't six weeks until that couple, who had been so committed to the church, suddenly found they had no time to go to church. They now had no time to sing in the choir, no time to practice, no time to study to teach the word of God. In fact, they slowly drifted out of the church. In that incident, that civic organization was wrong for that couple because it brought something between them and God and stole their dedication to Jesus Christ. Anything that takes your time away from the church may not be bad in itself, but if it comes between you and Jesus Christ it is wrong.

When the soldiers who accompanied Jesus Christ to the cross and while Jesus was dying on the cross, those men got on their knees at the foot of the cross and rolled dice for the robe of Jesus. There he was the perfect Son of God, there he was the Lamb of God slain from the foundation of the world. He was the only hope for time and eternity and those soldiers never looked up, they simply were doing those things which gratified themselves. That is exactly what people are doing in the world today. That is exactly what Christians are doing. God died on the cross in the person of the Son the Lord Jesus Christ. We pay no attention to him, we simply do those things which gratify our self and bring pleasure to ourselves. When God died for us, I think he had the right to plead with us to give him our love and our loyalty. What could be more natural than for a person who knows Christ as Savior to be in church? What less could he demand of us? Certainly, a man who died for us deserves our love and loyalty. When something steals that, it is wrong. I would hope to God and pray to God that the sins of the church members is not adultery, though some are guilty of that. I trust it is not the sin of drunkenness, though some are guilty of that as well. But the great sin of the church members is permitting things to come between them and Christ and the church. So the great sin of the Christian is worldliness. Things that may be good in and of themselves, but stealing slowly your time and your talent, your money and all the other things you ought to have committed to God, stealing them away from him. A fellow told me one time, brother, don't talk to me about coming to church. I can worship God on the golf course, or I can worship God on a boat fishing. I said that is true brother, but the fact is you don't. I guarantee you will hear God's name today on the golf course more than you will hear it at church, but it don't mean you are worshipping. You are thinking about increasing your score, or you are thinking about catching a fish. People just don't worship while they are fishing, I don't care what you say to me. I would encourage you to go fishing, but not on the Lord's Day.

The second great sin of the Christian is neglect. Neglect, first of all, to the Bible. God loved us with an eternal love and he wrote us a love letter. God's Bible is God's love letter to us and we let it lay unopened day after day, week after week, month after month and year after year. Simply neglecting the world of God is a sin. An African Chieftain invited an American to have dinner with him. The American saw in the chieftain's hut a Bible. So he began to make blasphemous remarks about that Bible and the Chieftain spoke up and said don't do that. Don't talk about the Bible. He continued to say, if it wasn't for that book, I would be eating you instead of you eating with me. And yet we neglect God's love letter to us. We neglect the claims of the church upon us. You know, I wish sometimes that Free Will Baptists believed a little more in salvation by works. I wish Free Will Baptist believed they had to go to church. The Church of Jesus Christ is the only institution founded on the face of this earth by Jesus Christ. When you accepted Jesus Christ as your personal Savior, you became a part of that glorious church. You have no right whatsoever to neglect its claims on your life. If you are too busy to go to church, you are busier than God ever intended you to be. When you neglect church, I don't care how good a Christian you are, you neglect something that keeps you in communion with God and in communion with one another. God designed the church to meet the needs of every Christian. In every church there are some people who quit. Some quit because, bless their hearts, they got their feelings hurt. The first seven or eight years of my ministry I spent more time solving hurt feelings than I did preaching the word of God. I got sick and tired of it and I quit. People think I don't care anymore. They think I have grown callus, but I have just got sick and tired of solving the hurt feelings of the saints of God. How can a person, who loves the Lord Jesus Christ, give way to his feelings in such a way that would cause him to turn his back on Christ's church? Some people quit church because someone hurt their feelings. I ask them this question: Did they ever spit on you when you went to church? Did they ever lash your back till it ran blood? Did they ever put a crown of thorns on your head and drive nails through your hands? They did Christ and he didn't quit. I'd be ashamed if I used that excuse to quit church. If you are the kind of man or woman who is always getting their feelings hurt, brother, your feelings need to get saved. You need to lay them at the feet of Jesus Christ.

Then there is the sin of ingratitude common among Christians. We are the most blessed people in the entire world. We ought to be the most thankful on God's earth. We never take time to thank him. Do you ever sit down and write a letter to someone who meant a lot to your life and just say I just want to tell you what you mean to me? Have you ever picked up the phone and called someone to tell them what they mean to you? I think sometimes the Lord is waiting to hear from us. I think he would like to hear us kneel and pray and say, Lord thank you for what you mean to me and what you've done for me. I have received a lot of nasty letters during my ministry. I received one that almost caused me to resign as pastor and leave the Free Will Baptist denomination. I mean it was a good one. I have gotten a lot of nasty letters and I've thrown them all away. I have gotten a lot of letters from people, believe it or not, that have been blessed and I've kept every one of them. Every once in a while at my desk, I take out those letters and begin to read them again. Just a note from someone who said I was particularly blessed by your visit, your prayer, your sermon, or something makes you feel good. What about God? When you got up this morning, you got up not only to a beautiful day, but you got up regardless of what your circumstances are, you got up to a way of life better than anywhere on the face of this earth. Millions are starving. Some have never heard of Jesus Christ. We live in the land of plenty and never pray and thank him. Someday when we come to the end of our life, we are going to look back and see how we have been blessed. Then we are going to say in shame, Lord I never thanked you for my blessed life.

There is one sin that I really need to talk about and that is the sin of a bad temper and intemperate language. Brother, it isn't easy when you get saved to rid yourself of a filthy tongue and a bad temper, but they have got to go. There is no excuse for anyone to use intemperate language. There might be a little excuse to lose your temper, but never to curse. The Bible says, he that ruleth his own spirit is better than he that taketh a city. You may not be guilty of the sin of the flesh. Maybe your sin is just flying off the handle. One lady said to me one time that was just the way she was. She said I get mad every once in a while and fly off the handle. That is just my nature. When God saved you he intended to change that and he would if you let him. You do more harm to your testimony and the church you are a member of by a bad temper and intemperate language than any sin of the flesh you can commit. Someone is looking at you and sees you at your work. They thought you were a Christian. They felt you were a pretty good example of a Christian. But one day they hear you when you fly off the handle and say something that is not right and they lose all respect for Christianity. You have done more damage than if they saw you drunk or if they saw you commit another sin of the flesh. General George Patton was said to have been one of the most profane men who ever lived. He had a chaplain who rebuked him for his profanity. George Patton said these words; "I do not know why I curse. I don't really mean to do it and I don't know why I do it, because I really am sincere in faith. I could not live a day without praying". Let me tell you something cursing and praying don't come from the same tongue. You can't curse God and then pray. You can't get an answer from God. Bitter and sweet don't come from the same stream and neither does cursing and praying. There are some people who need to get their tongues saved. There are some in church leadership roles that need to get their tongues saved and clean up their language. I've heard them speak and nothing breaks my heart worse than to hear a supposedly man of God tell an off colored joke or to use God's name in vain. There is no excuse for it. If you are guilty of that, you need to lay it at Jesus' feet and get forgiveness for it. God is hindering revival in you for that.

In closing, there is the sin of silence. A woman was killed on the streets of New York City with 38 people watching. When the police made their report, they found there were 38 eye witnesses to a murder and not one of them said a word, not one of them called out or called the police. They simply sat by and let a life be snuffed out and never said a word. That is unthinkable isn't it? They didn't care. At least they didn't care enough to get involved. People are lost all around us and I guess most Christians are guilty of this. Satan has his grip on people around us and they are on their way to hell and we as Christians say nothing. It would be like going to a home, seeing it in flames and know the family is in there asleep and say well I would wake them up but they might get mad. You go on your way, the house burns down and all of them perish. Folks are going to hell and we walk by and say nothing. We are silent with the whole world going to a lost eternity without Christ and it is a sin; sin of remaining silent. Christians are at ease in Zion. Christian have the attitude, well, I'm saved and on my way to heaven I really don't care about others. It may be your daughter, son, wife or husband that is lost. Tell them your concerns. Tell them that you are praying for them. Tell them that you are anxious for them, but don't be silent.

I told you about some sin of the saints. What should a Christian do if he is guilty of any of these sins? When your sin convicts you, you should do as David did when his heart was convicted of sin. Cry out to God in repentance. You have no other choice. There is no alternative, except to repent. Confess your sin; confess your laziness; confess your apathy and confess your indifference. Your calling as a Christian is, as the scripture says, if we confess our sins he is faithful and just to forgive us our sins and to cleanse us from all unrighteousness. Our churches need young people who are committed to Jesus Christ. We need young people who are committed to become ministers, missionaries, lay-workers of every kind. We need young people who are dedicated and committed to God. It seems that is what we are always aiming at, if somehow someway our young people could get on fire for God. Let me tell you what we need; we need a bunch of lazy older people to get dedicated to God. We need a bunch of people like me and you to clean up their act. We need a lot of older people to pray, confess their sins, to walk the streets as a man of woman of God in our town. People have said if you go out and get the lambs you may have a chance of getting the sheep. Go get the young people; go get the babies, teenagers and maybe the mom and dad will come. I say if you've got the sheep you automatically get the lambs. So let's not pray like a hypocrite; God do something for our young people. Let us pray this, when we are convicted of our sin, confess that sin and say God be merciful to me. God help me to be more dedicated, more consecrated. Help me to be a better Christian with a better testimony than what I've got. Help me to give my life to the church and to Jesus Christ. I feel the guilt myself in a lot of areas I could do better. Brother, if it convicts me it ought to convict you.

Prayer: Our Heavenly Father, we thank you again for this privilege of coming together. Father, we pray that you might help us, in love, receive admonition. Father, I pray, you would take the words that have been said. Help those of us who may be guilty to repent of our sin and confess our sin. We pray that you help us to not only preach in love but to respond in love and that we together as a church might grow spiritually in thy sight. Father, we pray that we might have a church where the adults are known for their commitment, their consecration, their holy living. We pray that our young people will be known for their vitality, beauty, strength and growth. Father, we've got a long way to go.

Many of us, as older people, need to confess on our knees before God, our failures as Christians. Together with our young people we need to stand and commit our lives to thee. I pray if there is one who does not know you as their personal Savior that they might kneel and receive Christ as their Savior. If there is a Christian that needs to make things right with you, I pray they come and confess their sin that you might be able to be just and to forgive them of their sin and cleanse them from all unrighteousness. Father, you know the needs of every heart, and pray you will meet them now.. For it is in his name we pray. Amen.

22

Giving: The Gift of Grace

II Corinthians 9

Whenever I feel a little bit down or a little bit discouraged, I preach myself out of that slump by talking about the grace of God. I want you to turn in your Bibles this morning to II Corinthians 9. In this particular chapter Paul is talking about giving. He is talking about every Christian ought to share that which he has, willingly and cheerfully, including his money. He ought to give in abundance to the needs of others so that he would be a blessing to other people and God could bless him. I don't want to talk about tithing or money, but in the asking to give cheerfully and to give bountifully that they might reap bountifully, Paul makes a wonderful and beautiful statement about our Lord. It is found in II Corinthians 9:8. "And God is able to make all grace abound toward you; that ye, always having all sufficiency in all things, may abound to every good work".

One of the facts that give so much difficulty to the world is the fact that Christianity is so beautifully given to us by God's revelation and all this grace and all of this Christianity was designed for sinners. It was designed for those that were lost; designed for those who had no hope; designed for those whom God loved and was willing to give his Son for. It was not designed for statesman, kings or presidents, but designed for sinners. It was designed for nobodies. The grace of God just came forth on humanity in a way in which we cannot comprehend. Now if the world could get that picture of God and that picture of Christianity, a lot of the problems we have today would no longer exist. For example, folks are always pointing to the church and saying those folks are not holy. Those folks live like we do. They are nothing but a bunch of hypocrites. How many times have you heard that or even said it yourself? When we begin to realize that by the grace of God Christians are not perfect; Christians never proclaim to be perfect; Christians never said they were better than anybody else. Christians have just faced the fact that they were sinners, on their way to hell and they reached out and got a hold of the grace of God. That's the only difference between church folks and those on the outside. They just partook of God's grace, that's all.

I saw a sign on the Assembly of God church the other day that stuck in my mind. It said, Christians are not perfect, just forgiven. Amen to that. The whole point of the Bible and the whole reason for God giving us this book from Genesis to Revelation was to show man's failure, not his perfection. God recorded from Genesis to Revelation the failure of man and God's provision for that failure. That is what the Bible is; God's provision for failure; God's grace for us all. God's gracious hope and salvation for the sinner is what God has revealed to us. The church is not a society of perfect people. In fact, we'd rather not have folks that were perfect in our church. In fact, our church is not perfect. There was an individual one time, who was looking for the perfect church, and they thought they had found the perfect church when they came to our church. They were disillusioned by that and went away seeking the perfect church. I said to that individual, please for God's sake and yours, when you find that perfect church don't join it because you are going to mess it up. You will ruin it if you get in it. The church is not an institution of perfect people, it is a community or fellowship of people who have experienced the grace of God. They have realized their sin and turned to Jesus Christ for help.

The failure behind all of that was what was behind the religious opposition to Jesus Christ. That's what finally nailed the Son of

God to the cross. The failure to realize what I just said. They saw Jesus coming and they said this man eats with sinners and fellowships with sinners and finally that failure to understand why he came, nailed him to the cross. Jesus said those who are whole need not a physician. I have come to seek and to save that which is lost. I have come to minister to him that is sick. I did not come to religious Pharisees, I came to save the lost. When they failed to realize that, they nailed him to the cross. Just like a sick man qualified for a doctor, the sinner qualified for Jesus Christ. There is not one in this church who would stand and say, I'm better than anyone else in town because I go to church. If there is, you are in the wrong place. You cannot say I'm better because I am a church member. All you can testify to is that you were lost, going to hell and God saved me. That is the only difference between us and the man outside. He is a lost sinner; I am a saved sinner. He's living in the world; I'm living by the grace of God.

There is a story in II Kings 5 which is a perfect picture of the whole experience that man has with God. II Kings 5:1 says "Now Naaman, captain of the host of the king of Syria, was a great man with his master, and honourable, because by him the Lord has given deliverance unto Syria: he was also a might man in valour, but he was a leper." That's a picture of Christianity. The picture of Naaman's cure is the picture of God dealing with man. Here was a man who was great, he was might and a man of valor. He was a brave man, who by him and through him, won their deliverance from the enemy. He was Mr. Walking Tall if there ever was one. But all of that greatness, intelligence and everything else was wiped clean by that last statement, "but he was a leper". Men and women are marvelous creatures. We have a marvelous mind and capacities. We are God's finest creation. We are something else. But all of our goodness and man has greatness, is wiped clean by the fact that he was a sinner. Leprosy is a type of sin. Here was a man who was great but was a leper. We are great in our ability and possibilities, but we are sinners.

In this predicament, this man had little sense. He called for the preacher and he asked him what can I do? That preacher gave him a very simple uncomplicated method of being healed and delivered from his predicament. Very simple, very beautiful and uncomplicated is the way God does things. He said to him go wash in the River Jordan and you will be healed. There is nothing simpler than that. It was too simple for this great man. Can't you just see this man, in all of his greatness, say they are going to bring a helicopter in and fly me to Mayo Clinic and have the best doctors in the world look at me and my name is going to be on the front page. But instead he saw a jeep pulling up to carry him to General Hospital. I can hear him say, surely you are carrying me to Mayo Clinic for I am a man of greatness. Don't give me some simple task to do, make it great. All you have to do Naaman is go wash in the River Jordan. Can't I go wash in some other river? Jordan is just a little muddy stream and there is no history to the River Jordan. At least, if I have to wash, let me wash in a river of importance. Then he called to his servant and the servant said to him a very wise thing. I want you to see the intelligence of this wise servant. He said, Master, if the man of God had told you to do some great thing would you have done it? He said yes. Then why not do this simple thing that he ask of you? Now that is Cheatham County philosophy if I ever heard it. It was so simple there was no getting around it. He couldn't by step it. He met a fact in the road and had to tip his hat to it. He realized the servant was right. It meant his salvation and God healed him in an uncluttered simple characteristic of God's way. It was so simple he almost missed it. God says to us today, you must realize that you are sinners then reach out and partake of God's provision for that and you will be saved. Most folks say give me a pledge card that I can put down how much money I'll give the church next year. I want to be baptized facing east at 7 a.m. Give me something that I must do. Don't tell me I can be saved by grace through faith. I want something challenging, something worthy of my character to come to God. God says my way is uncluttered and simple. My way is a gift and there is only two things you can do with a gift: refuse or accept.

Folks are stumbling over the same stone of not being able to see that God's way is so simple that a child can understand. That's why it is so beautiful. Men want something complicated; because men just will not accept anything but let me pay my own way. God says I'll not feed your ego or pride, salvation is a gift either receive it or reject it. Many turn away. For by grace are you saved through faith and that not of yourselves, it is a gift of God not of works should any man boast.

The word "grace" is a wonderful word. There are a number of scriptures that teach us the sheer beauty of the grace of God. Let me share some with you in closing. Ephesians 2:1 says, "And you hath he quickened, who were dead in trespasses and sins" We were dead; God gave us life, that's grace. Death for life is grace. Jesus so identified himself with us that he says in II Corinthians 5:21 "For he hath made him to be sin for us, who knew no sin; that we might be made the righteousness of God in him." Sin for righteousness, not ours, given to us that's grace. That is God's way. II Corinthians 8:9 "For ye know the grace of our Lord Jesus Christ, that, though he was rich, yet for your sakes he became poor, that ye through his poverty might be rich." Poverty for riches is grace. The Lord, creator of the universe became a pauper that you and I might enjoy the inexhaustible grace of God. He said to Paul, "for my grace is sufficient unto thee for my strength is made perfect in weakness. To change our weakness to strength is grace. It is not man's way but God's way. It is the opposite of what we would do if we were to work out our own salvation, but God's way is so simple. God's way is swapping all we need for what He is.

That is the economics of grace. To be made alive one must recognize that he is dead. To acknowledge that righteousness, one must confess guilt. To become rich, one must confess his poverty. To be strong one must confess his weakness. People say they want discipline. They want a to-do list. But folks want discipline on the wrong side of salvation. You find discipline on the other side of salvation not on this side. But to be saved is to simply say, Lord Jesus, I come, I admit my poverty, sin, death, my weakness and I come to thee. I give you all that I am, that I might become all that you are.

Prayer: Heavenly Father, we thank you for salvation and the plan of salvation. We thank you that it is so simple that the least of us could understand. Father, we thank you that you so ordain that we would be saved without works. There would be some of us who could not meet that qualification. We thank you Father that salvation is of grace. All we have to do is exercise our faith in what the scripture says about us and Christ. Then come to him and admit what you said about us is true. Then reach out and take your provision for our failure. Help us to confess our sin and need of thee. If there is one who does not know you as personal Savior I pray that they might bring all that they are, confess and repent their sin and turn and trust the Lord Jesus Christ. Father, I pray you will speak to Christians today. Strengthen and edify them and build them up in the faith and then challenge all of us. Touch hearts and do your work and may we be obedient to the wooing of the Holy Spirit. Bless your name and honor your Son in the name of Jesus we pray. Amen.

23

Be Sure Your Sin Will Find You Out

Numbers 32:23

"But if ye will not do so, behold, you have sinned against the Lord: and be sure your sin will find you out."

After having dealt with a group of the Israelites who did not want to cross over Jordan, but wanted to dwell on this side of Jordan in a place well suited for their lifestyle, the leader was quite upset. They ask permission that they might stay and not cross over into the promise land proper. The leader was upset because they asked such a thing. That they would be delivered from Egypt and go part of the way and not go all the way across Jordan and help their brothers in subduing and winning the land for themselves. They stood their ground and made their request on the basis that the men would cross over Jordan and fight as long as necessary with their brothers to insure their inheritance of the land and then they would come back to Jordan and raise their families. They were granted that permission. From Numbers 32:23 the words I want to use are the last words "... be sure your sin will find you out." This text does not teach that every sin we commit will come to light. It does not mean that every sin we commit will be found out. Most of us know that is not true because a lot of us are successful sinners. We have done things no one knows about yet. The text does not say every sin man commits will be found out and publicized but rather it is a statement concerning discovery of sin. Be sure your sin will find you out. Sin follows man. Sin is forever on the heels of man. Sin never sleeps. If we were to take a sinner or even one who is known to be a Christian and they are successful at their lives, they are beyond suspicion and no one knows that they are a hypocrite. Their sin has been covered from the eyes of the world, yet there has been something following them. That something which follows them is like a shadow. It's like a good fox hound that keeps trailing until that which follows the sinner will lay hold upon them and with a shot of triumph will shout, I have found you out.

Our text would let us know no man escapes from his own sin. Every sin we commit will haunt us and hunt us down, find you out and make you pay. There has never been one sinner who sinned and was successful eternally in that victory. You may escape being known, even escape the law of man, but the scripture says there is a law you cannot escape; the law of God and be sure your sin will find you out. There are several ways in which sin will find us out. I would like to briefly mention some to you today.

One of the ways our sin will find us out is, of course, in the execution of human laws. The longer I live, the more I realize the almost sacredness of our law and how much I realize the enforcement of those laws is necessarily important. It is amazing, the more we study, how sooner or later; a man who continually breaks the law is brought to book. He may be successful in evading the law for a while. All the time he is continually breaking the law of man, he is weaving around himself a net until finally sin will lay hold upon him and will say, I found you out. There are people who continually exceed the speed limit. They may drive for weeks and never get caught and then all of the sudden they get caught three times in one day. The first thing you know they have lost their license and insurance. The law finally takes hold upon him.

Secondly, Sin finds us out in a court where there is no bribing. Sin finds us out in the court of physical retribution of moral offenses. Our bodies pay for sin. That's not only true in certain vices where we know they are followed by serious and awful diseases, but it is also true in the general sense that holiness spills health and sin spills sickness. Why is it that we find so many men who have broken bodies and shattered intellect? Because of violated law. They continually broke the law of health and sooner or later that violation of breaking the law found them out and lay hold of them and they had to pay in that court of physical retribution for their sin.

Thirdly sin finds us out in our own character. You know when I started out a long time ago, I use to could tell the most successful lies of any boy in my community. I told some whoppers. I remember some of them. Folks began to believe me or they thought I was so silly that they wouldn't pay any attention and I thought they were believing me. Lying gets to be a habit. Sometimes we have to back up and change something because we've exaggerated. Have you ever noticed how somebody tells you something and it's just not right and you've got to fix it up a little before you tell it to the next fellow? Some folks just don't know how to tell something. So when I hear it I imagine how it would sound better, so we add to it. Then we have to go back and say that wasn't the way it was at all. Every lie we tell poisons that moral fiber of ours and under minds a moral constitution that we have. Every sin we commit breeds an ulcer in our character and it is far worse than one in our body. People use to think that a man could hire somebody and take advantage of them in their wages and be successful at it. Do you suppose any man gained anything by that? Do you suppose he gained more than that poor fellow he took advantage of lost? Do you think a man can over step a man in a business transaction and profit? Will he gain more than the other man loses? Every sin we commit and every advantage we take unfairly of another finds us out in our moral character. You cannot look at an obscene book, you cannot listen to a filthy story, and you cannot watch an R-rated movie without it having an effect on your soul. It will be a festering tumor in your own soul. Wherever your sin will find you out, it will find you out in your own character every time.

Sin will find you out in your own conscience. I am glad God so loved us and so constituted us that he gave us a conscience whereby if we are conscious of sin it is agony. I am glad when I sin I have no peace. I am glad when I sin and am conscious of sin it is hell on earth, until I get that sin forgiven or made right. There is absolutely nothing, there is not enough whiskey in the world or other pleasure, to soothe an aching conscience. Nothing will rid us of our aching conscience, except forgiveness. I still believe the best preacher that's ever preached a sermon was your own conscience. It is the best preacher God ever ordained. The very fact that our sin will find us out in so many places is proof positive that there is a moral governor of this universe. There is someone who created us and the earth who is a moral being. Have you ever noticed that everything in nature is attuned to virtue; to right? Have you noticed how everything in nature fights against that which is wrong and fights for that which is right? To see all of that and deny the fact of a literal moral God is the very height of ignorance. The very fact that our sin will find us out is proof that God exists.

Fifthly, sin find us out in our children. There is a fact in the Bible I wish was not there. I have read it many times. The Bible says God visits the sin of the father's upon the children into the 3rd and 4th generation of them that hate him. I don't like to think that God would do that, but it is a fact of the Bible that we have to face and you can't get rid of it by disbelieving it or getting rid of the Bible. The Bible reveals the fact and science has confirmed it. I talked to a young mother not too long ago. She was talking about the fact that she was proud, even though she was not a Christian that she was not a hypocrite. She was proud of the fact that she was a good mother. She made this statement, "I am totally honest with my children. When I pour me a drink, I pour one for my teen-age daughter. I don't hide it from her." I thought what an attribute to be proud of. She continued to say that she was proud of the fact that when she went to a party that she took her daughter with her and described the kind of party they attended. There is a philosophy today that no matter what you do as long as you are honest about it, it's alright. You find people who live in open adultery and people say at least they are honest about it. That doesn't cover up any sin. That does not make immorality right and it doesn't make adultery acceptable to God. To finish the story, I wondered a few years later when the young girl became the shame of the community because of her immorality, if that mother was still proud. So many people say, I've got children, but I'm not going to try and convince my children in their lifestyle. I'm not going to insist they go to church. I'm not going to insist they become a Christian; I'll just leave anything that deals with the spiritual realm up to my children. That too is the height of stupidity. Doesn't make any difference if you work with your children and they disappoint you. It doesn't make any difference if they don't pay you any attention. You still have that responsibility. There is still a promise in God's word that I hold on to and every other mom and dad can hold on to. If you train a child in the way he should go, when he is old he will not depart from it. I believe that wherever there is a child today that is out of God's will or out of his parent's will, God will never leave that conscience alone. God will never leave that heart alone. God will always and forever be on his case. Faithful is he that calleth thee, he will do it. I believe God honors his word. If you don't influence your children you can bet your home and all you have that the devil is influencing them every day. In fact, almost every moment of every day, the devil is influencing your children. If you don't influence your children, you've just turned them over to the devil and said have at him or her. Finally, your sin will find us in eternity. Sometimes we wish that death did end it all. But there is a life beyond the grave. I believe in that life we carry with us our sin and consequences of that sin. Somehow men's sin sometimes doesn't ever find them out in these other courts, but they will here. There is almost an obsession today with immorality, young men without character, entrap young girls who don't have a whole lot of sense and they are respected as the very finest of society. They are welcomed but it won't always be so. There is coming a time when they stand before the universe loaded with dishonor and will be cast into everlasting contempt. Men go through life despising God, laughing at his word, trampling under their foot the blood of his Son Jesus Christ and God let's them live. God's grace is extended to all. Nobody calls them into account, but it will not always be so. There is a world all of us are hurrying to and the Bible says in that our sin will find us out. All of that I mentioned is law. The law of God says that if a man sins it will find him out.

There is a remedy for all of that. There is no getting around it. The only escape from the unmerciful aspect of the law is found in the grace of the gospel of the Lord Jesus Christ. You see, sin was on our track as a wild animal would hunt us down and the Lord Jesus stood between us and that animal that was trying to trap us. God took my place and in his own body my sin and the punishment for that sin. He says to me, Come unto me. The Holy Spirit comes and ministers to us in such a wonderful way and helps us understand there is no hope for us outside the gospel. It lets us know there is hope for all of us. The Bible says. "...be sure your sin will find you out'. It will find you out in your conscience, your character, your children, your homes and in eternity unless you have taken God's provision for that, which is his Son.

Prayer: Our Heavenly Father, we praise you for who you are and for what you've done for us. We praise you, Father, that where sin did abound, the grace of God doth much more abound. We praise you that we can have victory over the penalty and power of sin. For you have made provisions for us to live a victorious life. Father, I pray we might face up to the fact that we are accountable. We are accountable for our actions unto our children, wives, husbands, neighbors and most of all we are accountable unto thee, a holy and righteous God. May we understand that there is a law in you which says if a man sins, his sin will find him out. Help us to escape the merciless law of retribution. Help us to find peace, forgiveness, and comfort in the grace of the gospel of the Lord Jesus Christ. We thank you for salvation and freedom we have as children of Thine. We thank you for what you have done for us, for that power you have put in our lives and for that new principle which you have given us to live by. In your name I pray, Amen.

24

The Old Time Religion

Acts 17:18-23

The Apostle Paul walked through the city of Athens. He knew the message the Athenians needed to hear. It was the message of how God sent His Son, the Lord Jesus Christ, how Jesus came born of a virgin, lived a life and then was crucified on the cross of Calvary, was buried and resurrected and He is coming again. That was his message. That was the only message Paul preached. The scripture says in verse 21 and it's a very picturesque statement: "for all the Athenians and strangers which were there spent their time in nothing else, but either to tell, or to hear some new thing". That is all they did all day long. I say to you their particular tribe is still among us. Those people who would do nothing except to hear or tell some new thing. Everywhere you go today and listen to people speak they are telling us we need a new system of government for example. The old one is outdated and needs to be brought into line with the modern age. There are those who say we need a new system of education, we need to change the old way of teaching. I've got the feeling that even though there are a lot of smart people in this world, we have more dumb ones. When they took the hickory stick and the three R's out of the school system, they didn't change it for the better. That may have been lacking, but they haven't replaced it yet with anything better. There are those who say we need a whole new system of marriage and divorce laws or we need a new economic system. Someone is always trying to tear down what we've got to replace it before they've got something better to replace it with.

The very worst of that tribe are those who say we need a new religion. That we need a new way of worshipping God. It needs to be brought up with this modern age in which we are living. The old way of worshipping is not sufficient in this day in which we live. We don't need a new religion. What we need is a better living. People talk about the old time religion and they talk about the new modern religion. I don't what they are speaking about really. I know we have made advances, I don't know that they are any better, but they are advances. We do meet in a building today that is air conditioned and comfortable. It has carpet on the floor and nice seats. We have baptisteries instead of creeks. People use buses to bring folks to church. We have all kinds of advances in the way we do things. Some have changed drastically. Some of our old traditions are not as binding as they once were and our customs have changed. But praise God, Jesus Christ is the same yesterday, today and forever. He never changes. He is the same Jesus Christ that Bro. Hudgens preached and some of the older preachers preached. It is the same Jesus that I preach to you today. He is still not willing that any perish but that all come to repentance. He is still willing to save whosoever will come unto Him. He that cometh unto Jesus He will in no wise cast out. He's the same Jesus.

When people talk about the old time religion, I can tell you what they are talking about. Some of you would like to know what the old time religion is because you have been worshipping this way all the time. When folks talk about the old time religion they are referring to that particular belief which believes that the Bible is the Word of God. In the modern religion, some folks say it contains the Word of God. The old time religion says this is God's book. From cover to cover it's God book: God breathed and God inspired. God gave the very words to put in this book. You know if you started to build a house and you got the doors from California, windows from Arkansas and you got the roof from

Kansas and it all came and fit together perfectly, you would say there is some master mind behind all this, guiding it and seeing to it that it all works out perfectly. God used 40 men over a period of 1500 years to write 66 books. When they finished it fit together perfectly. Everything that was shouted in the Old Testament was fulfilled in the New Testament. They fit together like hand and glove. Forty writers, 1500 years, 66 books and it all fits.

Why? Because it's God book. God breathed this book. The old time religion believes that this is God's book and God's way and God's only rule for faith and practice. A bunch of atheist met together one time to burn the Bible. They had a drunken party. They built a big fire and someone handed the loudest mouth atheist in the crowd the Bible and said, throw it on the fire, brother. He stood there for a moment and said, Fellows, let's not burn it unless we've got something better to take its place. There is nothing better. It is the only book. It is the only God inspired book. It is the only perfect book. When folks talk to you about errors in the Bible, do like my daughter did to me the other night. Christi left some food on her plate. This always worked when she was smaller. I said, there are kids going to bed tonight hungry in India. She said, name one. When folks tell you about all the errors that are in the Bible, say show me one. Brother, if we throw away this book we are lost forever. That's the first thing that old time religion is and what we as Free Will Baptist believe. Amen? We believe the Bible is God's book.

The second thing people talk about when they talk about the old time religion is a belief in the fact of sin. S-I-N, not human error, not human failings, not some upward stumble in man's progress, its sin. We believe in the fact of sin and man's lost condition. If you get sick and had a pain and went to the doctor, you'd say it hurts right here. The doctor knows that's not the problem and he will doctor you internally. When we look around the world today and see all the problems, we know it is not a surface problem. We know it is an eternal problem. We know that even people laugh at us the problem in the world today is sin. Greed is sin, isn't it? Political trickery is sin. People taking advantage of their neighbors is sin. Problems in the world is sin. The old time religion teaches us that it is sin. Sin entered the human family when Adam and Eve sinned in the Garden of Eden. That sin passed on to the human race. Because we have sinned, the Bible says, the wages of sin is death. The soul that sinneth, it shall die. Since we believe it is God's book, we believe what the book says. God's book says all those outside of Jesus Christ are lost in sin without hope in this world or the world to come.

A young boy went to a priest one day and confessed. He said, Father, I went out here to the street sign where the road forks. One goes to the swamp and one goes to town. He said I changed the sign around. A lot of folks ended up in the swamp. That is what the devil is doing. The devil is standing in the crossroads of life. He is giving out false directions. Many today stand in pulpits and preach errors. They preach some other gospel except the gospel which was delivered unto saints of God. It's pointing men to hell instead of heaven. I made this statement before and I make it again. There are "churches" in the world today who are sending more people to hell than they are to heaven. We believe in sin. We believe it was given to us in Adam and Eve's sin. We believe all men are sinners

When people talk about the old time religion, they believe in the virgin birth. We believe in the virgin birth, the divinity of Jesus Christ and the deity of Jesus Christ. We believe the gospel of Jesus Christ includes the miracles, it includes the resurrection. Some say Jesus was just a man, a good man, but just a man. We say He was God and man. He was the Godman. More than that he was born of a virgin and He was divine. He did what he did because He was God. The old time religion believes in the atoning of the blood of the Lord Jesus Christ because man is a sinner, and because he could not save himself. Because God was not willing for man to remain in that condition, God so loved the world that whosoever believeth in Him should not perish but have everlasting life. Jesus came and died on Calvary and shed his blood. Not because wicked men would silence his voice, but because He was God's sacrifice for sin. In that shedding of the blood there is atonement. The book of Hebrews says, without shedding of blood, there is no remission. Isaiah prophesied that he was wounded for our transgressions, he was bruised for our iniquity and God laid upon him the iniquity of us all. All we like sheep have gone astray, but God laid that sin, our sin, upon Him. He bore our grief and our sorrows. Paul said, you are not redeemed with corruptible things, but you were redeemed by the precious blood of the Lord Jesus Christ.

Now there is one thing the old time religion taught that we are getting weak on, brethren. We need, as Paul said to Timothy, to stir up your pure mind. The old time religion contained an expectancy and belief in the second coming of the Lord Jesus Christ. We believe He is coming again. Sometimes we just get lost and not hold it as dear as we ought to. We believe the second coming of the Lord Jesus Christ and we also believe in judgment, heaven and hell. Folks say, I see where there could be a heaven, but I don't believe in a hell. Where do you think they ever found out about heaven? Where did it come from? That's where you learn about hell. If you are going to believe part of it, believe it all, or believe none of it. On the Mount of Olives, when Jesus ascended into heaven, as the disciples stood there gazing as He went out of sight. The men in white came and said to those disciples, why stand ye here gazing into the heavens. This same Jesus, which you saw go away shall come again in like manner. We believe that. We believe there has to be a judgment. We believe there are two judgments. We believe there is a Great White Throne Judgment, which every unbeliever will stand before. We believe there is the Judgment Seat of Christ where every Christian will stand before and receive the crown of life, the reward of serving the Lord Jesus Christ.

Yes, I believe in a heaven and a hell. The scripture says, in my Father's house are many mansions. That's heaven. It also said, whosoever was not found in the Lamb's Book of Life was cast in the lake of fire. That's hell. There has to be a judgment. There has to be a heaven and a hell.

That's the old time religion. The belief in the word of God as being the inspired word of God. Is it sufficient? Do we need to change it? Is it sufficient for the age in which we live? The old time religion is still powerful. The old time gospel is powerful. It has the power to transform lives. Remember in the New Testament when John came to Jesus and Jesus called him son of thunder. He was the kind of man that wanted God to call down fire. He told Jesus, don't talk to those folks anymore, call down fire and kill them all. Jesus called him son of thunder but then the Holy Spirit began to mold John. The Holy Spirit began to love John, change John and then we hear John saying, little children love one another. Nothing but the old time religion can cause that to happen to a man. Did you know that? Only old time religion can cause a man to be changed like that. Zacchaeus was a stingy crook. When he met Christ, he said these words: I'll sell all that I have and give half to the poor and if I have cheated anyone in my past, I will give them four times what I took from them. Brother, when a man gets hit in the pocketbook he's saved. When Zacchaeus hit the ground, his pocketbook fell out wide open. What could change a man like that? What could change a money hungry, grabbing, stingy Jew into a man who said, I'll give all I got. Only old time religion can change a man like that.

Peter was an impulsive outspoken cursing fisherman. He met Jesus and he denied the Lord Jesus Christ. On the Day of Pentecost, when the power of God got a hold of Peter, we hear him preaching a very simple message and we saw 3,000 souls being saved. What could happen to a cursing fisherman to make him a preacher of the gospel of the Lord Jesus Christ? Nothing but the old time religion can change a man like that. You see people whose lives have been transformed. You're life has been transformed, I'm sure. If it hasn't been transformed or changed, you better check up on your experience with Jesus Christ because when Christ comes into your life, He changes everything there is to change. This includes your relationship with one another.

Brother, I believe the gospel is still powerful to save. I believe it will help you to live and help you to die. I believe there is no substitute for old time religion. Folks say, well I believe in this modern age, we ought to live under the philosophy of let your conscious be your guide. You know what's wrong with that? The Bible says there is a way that seemeth right unto men, but the end thereof is death. Follow your conscious and it seems the right way, but the Bible says the end of all that is death.

Some folks say we need more idealism. That won't save you. Folks say we need more sincerity. That won't save you. We need more folks who believe in being good and moral. That's true but it won't save you. There is only one thing that can cleanse you from sin. Only one thing that can help you in time of death, to stand with you in the time of judgment and that is the shed blood of the Lord Jesus Christ. Jesus is all we need. Jesus is the great physician. If you need help, he's the doctor. If we need education, Jesus said, I am the truth. If we need someone to comfort us, Jesus said, my love will never leave you and I'll never forsake you. If we are sorrowful, he says, come unto me all ye that labor and are heavy laden and I'll give you rest. He is all we need.

The old time religion is sufficient for everybody. Do you know Jesus, who was born of a virgin, who died for your sin? Do you know Jesus who was buried and was resurrected by the power of God? Do you know the Jesus who ascended into heaven and will one day come again. Do you know Him?

IN MY FATHER'S WORDS

25

Where Will You Spend Eternity?

Matthew 25:31-46

I am going to ask you a question that I was asked many years ago. It made me mad when it was asked of me and it may make some of you mad. But if it has the same results in years to come as it did me, I shall profit from asking the question.

Matthew 25:31-46: "When the Son of man shall come in his glory, and all the holy angels with him, then shall he sit upon the throne of glory: And before him shall be gathered all nations: and he shall separate them one from another, as a shepherd divideth his sheep from the goats: And he shall set the sheep on his right hand, but the goats on the left. Then shall the King say unto them on his right hand, Come, ye blessed of the Father, inherit the kingdom prepared for you from the foundation of the world: For I was a hungred, and ye gave me meat: I was thirsty, and ye gave me drink: I was a stranger, and ye took me in: Naked, and ye clothed me: I was sick, and ye visited me: I was in prison, and ye came unto me. Then shall the righteous answer him, saying, Lord, when saw we thee a hungred, and fed thee? Or thirsty, and gave thee drink? When saw we thee a stranger, and took thee in? Or naked, and clothed thee? Or when saw we thee sick, or in prison and same unto thee? And the King shall answer and say unto them, Verily I say unto you, Inasmuch as ye have done it unto one of the least of these my brethren, ye have done it unto me. Then shall he say unto them on the left hand, Depart from me, ye cursed, into everlasting fire, prepared for the devil and his angels".

I want you to notice the last verse, verse 46 which gives us two statements concerning eternity. There is an eternal blessing and eternal life and there is an eternal death. I want to ask you today a question to your face honestly whether you are a Christian, unsaved, atheist or whatever you call yourself. That question is, where will you spend eternity? I want all of you to answer it right now. Where will you spend eternity? You will spend it somewhere, where will that somewhere be? The first time a preacher asked me that question I said very rebelliously in my heart, it's none of your business where I shall spend eternity. Then when I thought better of it I said, I don't know where I will spend eternity, no one knows where he will spend eternity. But God showed me in his word that you can know. There is no reason to doubt. You know today where you are going to spend eternity. You know you will either spend it with God or you will spend it with the devil in hell.

There are a lot of big words in the Bible. There is a word "God" which is everything. There is the word "Christ" that all our hope is wrapped up in. The word "lost" which tells us of the tragic result of living a life without God and going on without receiving Jesus Christ as our Savior. In our text, there are two big words: everlasting and eternity. I wish I could say those words with such power and clarity that every listener would see the tragic condition of a lost soul. I wish I could say "lost" and it would grab people's heart. I wish I could say "lost throughout eternity" and it would move people with compassion and conviction to see what is wrapped up in the term. A thousand years from now every one of you will be somewhere. Ten thousand years from now, where will you be?

A cobbler had a clock on a shelf behind his machinery and in the quite time he was working on the sole of those shoes that pendulum would swing back and forth in that clock. He began to think as that pendulum would begin to swing and he would say, eternity where, eternity where and he could not get rid of that thought. And the only way he could get rid of that haunting change of that clock was when he accepted the Lord Jesus Christ as his Savior and the taunting went away, for he knew where he would spend eternity. He knew he would spend it with God himself. I wish I could get that thought in your heart today. I wish I could get that taunt: eternity where, eternity where into your heart so deeply that you would be sure you are ready to meet God. Not too long ago a house was on fire and the lady of that house rushed to a room and recovered her jewelry. She fled the house and let her baby burn to death the next room. People today are trifling with the things of the world and neglecting the most valuable possessions of all and that is an eternal soul that all of us possess. People are not ready to die. People are not ready to live. People are not ready to face the judgment. Folks, are you ready to face eternity?

Let's think for a moment about the length of eternity. How long is eternity? It begins where human computation ends. If you think in your mind and travel back to millions of years before there was ever an earth, before there was a star or moon. If you could think back to the endless ages of the past, you could not even begin to think about God's eternal existence. But when you think back as far as you can in your mind that is eternity past. When you think ahead of all the generations that shall come if the Lord tarries, you are talking about eternity future. But there is no way to compute the beginning and end when there is no beginning and no end. Then eternity means forever and forever without end and without beginning. I am amazed at what folks tell us. People can study the stars and can tell you their name and when they are going to move and where they will be ten years from now. Some of you were alive when Haley's comet made a trip across the sky in 1910. Haley's comet streaked the skies in 1910 and came again in 1985 and will come again in 2061. They can tell you the position of stars a hundred or thousand years from now, but they can't tell you how long eternity is. They can tell you many things but they cannot tell you about eternity.

There is a cave in Kentucky that they have tried to measure. They have never been able to find the bottom of that cave. Neither can they tell you the length of eternity. The only answer to how long is eternity comes to us from one statement from the Word of God. "The peace of the righteous is everlasting and the doom of the wicked is without end". The state of the righteous is peaceful without end and the doom of the wicked is without end.

What is eternity? Someone wrote, what is eternity? on the blackboard. A girl went up and underneath the statement she wrote it is the life of the almighty. What is eternity? It is the life of the almighty. God is omnipotent which means he had the power to create all things. He had the power to create a never ending eternity. The ability to create time that never ends. Because he is omnipotent and can do that means he is omniscient. He has the knowledge to do that. He is omnipresent which he can fill that eternity forever. He is eternal. Before the world was ever formed and the moon ever shone and the stars ever twinkled, before there was a tree, or rain or a river that flows, God was. When the sun refuses to shine, and the moon goes dark and the rivers run dry, God will still be alive. God will live forever – he is eternal. Eternity is the life of the Almighty. When we talk about the character of God and the attributes of God, we learn a little about eternity itself.

What will be the conditions of eternity? What will be the condition of the child of God in eternity? The child of God will be home. He will be in the place he was created to be in in the first place, before sin entered the human race. In eternity, the child of God will be at home. He will be in God's dwelling place called heaven. He will be home with the Savior. He will be in a place where there is no sorrow. Can you imagine being in a place where there is no misunderstanding or problems in our emotions or spirit, no tears, no graves on the hillside of glory. We will be home forever and forever with God. If you were to take the sweetest moment you ever experienced and multiply that by a billion you would see what one moment in heaven would be like. When we've been there ten thousand years bright shining as the sun, we will have no less days to sing his praise than when we first begun. Amen? That will be the condition of the saved in eternity.

What about the condition of the lost? The Bible says that they will be in hell forever. Having gone through life without Jesus Christ, having come to the end of their life without hope, our sin, will send us to hell. It is not God's fault. If a man goes to hell, it is not because God sent him there, but because of his own sin he chose to go there. God did not prepare hell for us. He prepared it for the devil and his angels, yet man insists upon going to a place he was never supposed to go. He insists upon rebelling against God. He insists upon climbing over everything God puts in his way, to climb and fight his way into hell. The only way a man gets to hell, is he has to climb over the prayers of his mother and father, he has to climb over every gospel church in the community, every gospel song, over every testimony and over every gospel sermon. On and on he has to climb over all of that to get to hell. It will not be God's fault. He shall spend eternity separated from God, destined to spend eternity in doom and remorse.

Why do we give so much consideration to eternity? We consider it because we are interested in our future life. Ever since the first man walked the face of the earth, there has been that conviction in the heart of man that death does not end it all. The grave does not end it all. Man has always believed he shall live again. From the natives of Africa to the Indians of the American plains, there has always been that belief, I shall live after death. What put that thought there? Is it because man is selfish and says, I'm man and so surely one life is not enough, so somewhere in this universe, I'll live again. No, God put that eternal life in man. God put that spark that he should live forever in man. Man always had the conviction that he would live again. We are interested in it because we know we shall live again. But the amazing thing is because all of us believe that and are convinced we shall live again, yet how few ever do anything to prepare for it. Isn't it rather strange that we can be so indifferent about something that so saturates our being as living again. It is a tragic thing to gamble with eternity knowing that all men shall face the judgment. Most people intend to go to heaven. They intend to get their heart right with God, but they gamble that they have one more day left to live. They are going to live it for themselves. They are going to live it for Satan. Gambling all the time that God will not call them home today. Tomorrow I will take care of it. We keep moving that up one day at a time until the devil has blinded our hearts and minds and God speaks and our hearts stop and we go off into eternity unprepared to meet God.

It is a tragic thing to gamble with one's eternal soul. If you died right this moment and the hand of death gripped your heart and it stopped this moment, where would you go? Where would you spend eternity if you died this moment? You would spend it somewhere. In a fleeting moment, your soul would go somewhere. Do you know the Savior than can alone save your soul? We consider it because we're not very reckless with our best possessions. Whenever I get as much as a dollar, which is every now and then, I put it in the bank. I don't entrust it to a stranger. I'm not reckless with life, I don't think. I don't play with rattlesnakes. I don't run into houses that are on fire. I am not reckless with my life. Now my wife thinks I travel to close to the cars in front of me and someday I'm going to get smashed. But other than that I am not reckless with this life of mine.

But the soul is more important than that. Why are we so careless? I consider eternity because this is the place to prepare for. There is no such thing as preparing for it after you leave here. This is the place of preparation. Do you ever notice when a famous person dies there is a write up in the paper about how popular he or she was, how rich he was, how much following he had, but never a statement about his relationship with God.

Why? Because they don't think it is important. In the thinking of the world, that relationship between man and God is not important. What shall it profit that man when he stands before God having not made any preparation for eternity? What shall profit a man, if he gain the whole world and lose his own soul?

Let two men die; one be an invalid and one be a strong man. Let the invalid believe in the Lord Jesus Christ and let the strong man live for the devil. What good is strength in hell? Let one rich man and one poor man die. The poor believed in God and the rich man lived for the devil. What good will riches be in hell? One educated man and one ignorant man die. I am not against education. I wish I had some of it myself. Let the ignorant trust in God and the educated live for the devil. What good will education do in hell? Someone said I'd rather be learning the English alphabet in heaven than study Greek in hell?

Where will you spend eternity? You alone can answer that question? The Lord gives you the choice. Man has a free will and has the right to choose and the ability to choose. Is Christ crowded out of your life? Has Christ been divorced from your business? Have you built your home without him? Are you rearing your children without him? Where will you spend eternity? God loves you and Christ died for you. The Holy Spirit is here to convince you to begin your eternity with him today.

www.ingramcontent.com/pod-product-compliance
Lightning Source LLC
Chambersburg PA
CBHW060918040426
42445CB00011B/686